This is number two hundred and twenty-three in the
second numbered series of the
Miegunyah Volumes
made possible by the
Miegunyah Fund
established by bequests
under the wills of
Sir Russell and Lady Grimwade.

'Miegunyah' was Russell Grimwade's home
from 1911 to 1955
and Mab Grimwade's home
from 1911 to 1973.

The Contemporary Australian Writers Series explores and articulates the significance of select Australian writers' literary works.

Contributors to the series act as both guide and critic, illuminating how literary works make and remake worlds—reimagining histories and futures, communities and institutions, families and homes. In doing so, the series recognises the unique role of the artist in shaping our perception of the world around us and, in the act of reading and critique, ourselves.

The series brings to the fore a public discussion of the value of the local in an international literary culture, and celebrates those writers whose work has moved us, enlightened us and surprised us.

London

CONTEMPORARY AUSTRALIAN WRITERS

London

Tanya Dalziell

Melbourne University Publishing acknowledges the traditional owners of the unceded land on which we work, learn and live: the Wurundjeri Woiwurrung peoples of the Kulin Nation. We pay respect to elders past, present and future, and acknowledge the importance of Indigenous knowledge.

THE MIEGUNYAH PRESS
An imprint of Melbourne University Publishing Limited
Level 1, 715 Swanston Street, Carlton, Victoria 3053, Australia
mup-contact@unimelb.edu.au
www.mup.com.au

First published 2024

Cover design by Evi O. Studio
Text design and typesetting by Cannon Typesetting
Printed in Australia by McPherson's Printing Group

A catalogue record for this book is available from the National Library of Australia

ISBN 9780522879032 (paperback)
ISBN 9780522879049 (ebook)

Series Editor: Melinda Harvey

For Jamie

Contents

Introduction

By her own admission, Joan London is a slow writer. Across a career spanning over forty years, she has published two original short story collections, *Sister Ships* (1986) and *Letter to Constantine* (1993), and three novels *Gilgamesh* (2001), *The Good Parents* (2008) and *The Golden Age* (2014), with the occasional short story punctuating those months, even years, of what she nominated very early on in her writerly life as 'prepared waiting'.[1] Yet, to measure only in numbers London's contributions to Australian literature seems limited. There are other markers: the awards and shortlistings her writing has consistently attracted, for example, and London herself being honoured by the state government of Western Australia as a 'State Living Treasure' in 2015; or the translations of her writings into multiple languages including Chinese, Spanish, Portuguese, Italian and French. And then there is what this volume in the Contemporary Australian Writers series hopes to offer, which is a concentrated, extended engagement with her short stories and novels to reflect on London's artistry; to recognise the original contributions London's writing has made to Australian culture; and to listen in on the conversations her work has with its own changing times.

London was born in 1948 and has spent much of her life in the port town of Fremantle in Western Australia. A number of the women of her approximate generation who also turned to writing are now household names, having made significant and lasting impacts on Australian literature and society. Remembering that the expatriate writer Shirley Hazzard, only one generation earlier, had determined Australia to be 'a remote, philistine country … and very much a male country, dominated by a defiant masculinity that repudiated the arts',[2] First Nations author Sally Morgan, Blanche D'Alpuget, Amanda Lohrey, Waanyi writer Alexis Wright, Kate Grenville, Gail Jones, Nadia Wheatley, Di Morrissey and Helen Garner, among others, have rightly attracted respect and admiration.

London has arguably had a lower profile, working in a Fremantle bookshop and stepping into sight with the release of each of her books. These have been generously reviewed and loudly praised by other authors. Canadian short-story writer and winner of the Nobel Prize for Literature, Alice Munro, has celebrated London's work, declaring her stories 'felt, alive—such grace and sharpness together',[3] and Australian novelist Charlotte Wood has admitted: '*The Good Parents* is the only book I've ever truly wished I had written myself'.[4] More recently, Wood has suggested that when writing her latest book, *Stone Yard Devotional* (2023), 'one of the people I thought about … was Joan London, a writer I absolutely adore and admire':[5] *Stone Yard Devotional* might be thought of as Wood's complement, and compliment, to the London novel she longs to have written insofar as it, too, is preoccupied with what it means to be 'good'.[6] Despite the international reach of London's work and its influence on the next generation of Australian writers, London's writing has largely escaped the attention of literary scholarship. This circumstance is reflected by the presentation to London of the Patrick White Award in 2015, a prize that was first given in 1974 to Christina Stead and recognises important writers who have not received commensurate recognition. Elizabeth Webby, esteemed scholar of Australian literature, has puzzled at this circumstance:

> Although each of [London's] books has won at least one award and been shortlisted for many others, they have attracted little in the way of extended critical response.
>
> That's even more surprising when one thinks how rare it is for a fiction writer to be equally good at short stories and novels. Most of the great writers of short fiction, such as [Anton] Chekhov, Katherine Mansfield and Henry Lawson did not publish longer works. The fiction of [Tim] Winton and David Malouf, who have also published acclaimed novels and stories, has attracted several book-length studies as well as numerous critical essays.
>
> Why has London been neglected? Is it that her novels and stories are less recognisably Australian than Winton's and Malouf's? They do not deal with big national stories or iconic landscapes, and have tended to focus on female rather than male characters.[7]

London has not been neglected by the reading public; her writing has attracted strong and enthusiastic interest from both national and overseas audiences. And the critical forgetting or side-lining of London seems counterintuitive given that her stories enlarge our understandings of Australian culture and its literature. Rather than admitting expectations for Australian narratives—those 'big national stories or iconic landscapes', for example—London's works exercise priorities of their own that are responses to the time of their writing and have continuing relevance and significance. The focus of the *The Golden Age* on both a traumatised Hungarian-Jewish family seeking to rebuild a postwar life in Perth, Western Australia, and the capacity of art—music, poetry—to remember and to hope speaks to the time it represents as much as it does the time in which it was written and continues to be read. The sympathetic interest taken by *The Good Parents* in the dissolution of youth's idealism not only represents generations of an Australian family but is also a meditation on shared experiences of change, set as it is on the cusp of a new millennium. *Gilgamesh*'s protagonists are peripatetic, presuming to roam the world in a way that is very different from the forced relocation of the family central to *The Golden Age* but nevertheless also registers deeply the horrors both wide-reaching and intimately experienced of the violence repeatedly done to others. The short stories burrow equally into dreams unbounded by national borders or reason and the realities of Australian women, mothers, daughters and lovers in times when those roles are under pressure. Collectively, London's writing is an ensemble of responses to and anticipations of the world around it, and this eclectic scope is reflected in its form.

One of London's under-recognised strengths and contributions to Australian literature is her patient capacity to build complex narrative worlds populated by numerous characters and storylines. London pictures life in Australia and transnationally in terms of generational change, interwoven with questions about the responsibilities people have to one another across cultures and time; her work is not interested at all in national mythmaking but instead is attuned to ethical interconnectedness. As such, London's writing turns not on individuals, one of the conventional building blocks of the novel, but on relationships: intimate ones between lovers; ambivalent ones between parents and children; and Australian literature's relationships with, and obligations to, its histories, social contexts and the shifting world beyond its borders.

London herself has recognised how her writing registers wider cultural change. Twenty years ago, London noted:

> to prepare for the publication of my Collected Stories [*The New Dark Age* (2004)], I had to read over the stories from my first two collections, which I hadn't done for a long time. The first book was published in 1986 and the second in 1993 and I was struck by how much, in small details, everyday life has changed. The average person didn't have a mobile phone, or a computer, or an air conditioner and if you went overseas you didn't phone home, you wrote aerogrammes.[8]

And during a presentation she gave in China around the same time, London related how these small details exist alongside necessary, significant transformations in Australia and the world:

> These are times of great change for Australians. Our vision of ourselves and our place in the world is changing ... the past decade has been *troubling* for many Australians. Not only because of our involvement in the 'war on terror', with troops sent to Iraq and Afghanistan but also because of our treatment of refugees, mainly of Middle-Eastern and Muslim descent who have attempted to find asylum in Australia.

> It was also the time of the release of *The Stolen Generations Report* [*Bringing Them Home* (1997)], about white Australia's cruel treatment of our own Indigenous people ... treatment which the general public was no longer able to forget or ignore. It was as if *the secrets of our history* had come out into the open.
>
> There has been a lot of *soul-searching* amongst some Australians. *Who are we*? Our old vision of ourselves as easy-going, humorous, egalitarian, fair-go for all, help-your-mate people just won't stick anymore. Like all stereotypes, it's never really been true.[9]

Arguably, these conditions continue to inform our own century with their still oftentimes unanswered urgencies. And London's writing enacts ongoing 'soul-searching' not only in terms of personal introspection but also in its querying how we live in a world of cruelty and fear, of beauty and expectation.

Adjacent to these concerns that London's narratives express, her career says something instructive too about 'Australian literature' itself and throws light on London's place in Australian letters. London's experience of studying English literature and French at The University of Western Australia in the late 1960s and early 1970s, for instance, is a reminder that Australian literature itself is a relatively recent invention:

> I wasn't taking a course on Australian literature—there wasn't one. Even though I enrolled in a course called The Modern Novel and was reading James Joyce and Ford Madox Ford—Virginia Woolf was the only female writer to merit a mention—I rarely read literary journals and had no real idea about the literary culture of my own country.[10]

It was not that 'Australian literature' did not exist until some time after London graduated. Rather London's anecdote highlights that her own writing of short stories, from the early 1980s, coincided with an exerted cultural effort to recognise and value not only Australian literature as such but (largely non-indigenous) women's writing as well. As London reflected, in another context:

> I think that I have been very lucky, in that by the time I was writing seriously, and publishing, there was a lot of extremely strong women writers, and this was inspiring and encouraging. I feel too that I have mopped up the benefits of feminist critics in my own acceptance of the essentially female content of my own work.[11]

In addition to her own talent and commitment that developed alongside other 'strong women writers', another significant foundation of London's achievements was her original publisher, Fremantle Arts Centre Press, and what it heralded for writers in Western Australia.[12] By the time London published in 1986 her first short story collection, *Sister Ships*, the small publishing house, underwritten by state government grants, had been in operation for eleven years. Its explicit aim was the publication and promotion of Western Australian writers and local 'regional writing' because of the reasonable perception and experience at the time that authors at some distance geographically, and possibly psychologically, from the mainstream publishing houses centred in Sydney and Melbourne, found it difficult to get a foothold in those arenas, let alone access to their markets. (The mental separation is quite likely exaggerated: a flick through *Fremantle Arts Review*, a publication associated with Fremantle Arts Centre Press and an enlightening window into the local writing scene, unsurprisingly suggests a sustained interest in national literary activity, with reviews of books by Garner, Grenville, Olga Masters, Frank Moorhouse, Janine Burke and Jean Bedford, to name only a few.) But as London came to realise:

> Being West Australian had not after all turned out to be a disadvantage: in fact, it had become a sort of advantage, because at the same time I had started to write, the Fremantle Arts Centre press had been established … and by the time I came to publish, it was a confident, thriving and highly regarded small press, which had established the reputations of writers such as Elizabeth Jolley, and published a national best seller, [Albert Facey's] *A Fortunate Life* … For the first time, there was speculation that isolation from the distractions of the literary world was perhaps a good thing. The effect of the Fremantle Arts Centre Press on West Australian writing has been immense. Contrary to my impression as a child, it became obvious that books *were* being written in Western Australia.[13]

London had significant impact on the publisher, too. *Sister Ships* won *The Age* Book of the Year in 1986; the newspaper hosting that prize later reflected that 'this was an extraordinary coup for a book by an unknown author with a print run of just 1500, published by a small Western Australian company'.[14] And the surge in demand for copies of the short story volume at once exposed the fragility of the press's distribution arrangements. It prompted Penguin Books to approach Fremantle Arts Centre Press with a comprehensive national agreement. And the Press, in turn, continued, and continues to this day, to play a significant part in promoting not only books 'written in Western Australia' but the very idea of Western Australian writing and writers, including London and her short stories, which are certainly not uniformly 'about' Western Australia.

London genuinely shares the local identification the press rests on and promotes. At writers' festivals and other public events London has spoken of her attachments to Western Australia and to Fremantle in particular, where she was not only first published but where she continues to live with her husband Geoffrey after bringing up their daughter and son, and becoming grandparents. Fremantle was also 'the first port where all [her] grandparents arrived'.[15] And each of London's three novels is at least partly set in Western Australia: the fictional south-west town of Nunderup in *Gilgamesh* takes its cue from the historically (in colonial terms) dairy farming region of Margaret River; *The Good Parents* features a fictional Western Australian wheatbelt town (loosely based on Wagin); and *The Golden Age* is set in Western Australia's capital city, Perth. But London has also said that she 'never set out to be a "West Australian" writer'.[16] It is an acknowledgement consistent with a healthy scepticism about stereotypes and easy categorisation that runs through her writing. And perhaps it also suggests a playful aspect to London's notion that living and writing where she has for most of her life—she did spend some time in Melbourne working on *The Golden Age*, and much earlier lived in England for a period—is somehow apart from 'the literary world'. After all, London is fully immersed in the realm of ideas and imagination that reading affords, and her literary influences are registered in her writing in ways that complicate any convenient conception of her as a regional writer.

This breadth is worth underlining as reviewers of London's writing often compare it to the work of Alice Munro. This connection is most likely made because London herself has repeatedly mentioned her admiration of Munro: dislocation, London suggests, is a 'source of the texture of her [Munro's] work, the density of reference to the physical world, the attempt to capture the spirit of a place or person or feeling, of what Virginia Woolf called "the thing in itself"'.[17] And as part of an invited talk at the Vancouver Literary Festival in 2009 to celebrate Munro's work, London told her audience: 'Alice Munro has been the most important influence in my writing life … Her stories make me think of all the stories in my life that I've left untold'.[18] In turn, and in addition to Munro praising London's work—most likely recognising the two authors' shared appreciation of Chekhov—the orbits of each have intersected at international writers' festivals over decades. Yet, there are as many differences between and within London's individual short story collections and books as there are similarities, and Munro's works are equally diverse. So, while the suggestion that London's writing recalls Munro's is no doubt apt, it also risks smoothing out the specificities and complexities of each of these authors' texts. And it can also downplay other influences, in addition to Munro, important to London's writing.

The authors that Fremantle Arts Centre Press was publishing during the 1980s and 1990s—Philip Salom, Elizabeth Jolley, Brenda Walker, Marion Campbell, John Kinsella and Gail Jones, for example—constituted a loose writerly community for London. Drusilla Modjeska, an author as well as London's friend, proved to be a wonderful, supportive editor: on reading the first draft of *Gilgamesh*, for example, Modjeska recognised its value immediately when London herself was unsure and encouraged the short story writer to develop it and to rethink the novel's original ending.[19] And alongside this practical, personal support is the writing of others, especially (but not exclusively) short story authors. The American William Maxwell, with his focus on small-town America in short stories that are willingly attendant to leaving 'so much ... completely unexplained and unaccounted for',[20] is another significant influence for London and an author with whom she shares a concern for the inexplicable. London also cites the importance of the work of English novelist Penelope Fitzgerald, who is heralded as 'a great model if you want to think about historical research. She's a wonderful writer ... She's very important to me actually. Very',[21] underscoring London's enduring commitment to a specific form of realism.

This realism is of a different order to that of the late nineteenth-century *Bulletin* 'bush' writers, among whom Henry Lawson is counted, which came to be aligned with an ethos of egalitarianism and (at times jingoistic) nationalist sentiment, and was oftentimes set in opposition to artistic experimentation. London's realism instead continues the expression it found in the writings of Elizabeth Harrower, and in particular in Harrower's last book, *The Watch Tower* (1966). Set in postwar Sydney, that novel grapples with the psychology of gendered suffering (a theme to which London's admirer, Charlotte Wood, would turn and make her own in the novel, *The Natural Way of Things* (2015)).[22] Harrower was a mid-twentieth-century novelist whose work, perhaps like that of London's, was seen as confounding in light of the dominant expectations of Australian literature of her time, and 'even when it was positive, the critical reception of this novel was tentative, and soon ended in uncertainty and silence'.[23] Webby's querying about the critical silence around London's writing uncannily echoes the fate of Harrower's narratives, especially when London's appraisal of *The Watch Tower* in her introduction to the 2012 re-issuing of the book by Text Publishing, is couched in terms that could as easily be applied to her own narratives: 'Something runs clear and strong through this wonderful, painful novel, the dark and the light. The victim and the survivor. Suffering and joy. The knowledge of both. *Reality*.'[24] Rather than its subject—London does not specialise in the slow cruelty Harrower has her female characters endure—this melding of the aesthetic and the material, the simultaneous holding together of what could otherwise be conceived of as mutually exclusive, and the idea that fiction might be a site where the complexity and a truth of life is grasped, however fleetingly, are vital components of both London's and Harrower's realism.

Equally important for the realism of London's work is historical excavation and a concern with the minutiae of her narrative worlds. The fine detail given to places and times in London's novels makes this commitment clear and is also witnessed by her literary archive. This record consists of small sheets of paper that seem to have caught the corner of ruminative moments; a plethora of sticky notes often containing one line, or one idea.[25] There are notebooks, too, filled with historical and 'background information', which suggests London's concern for both empathy and accuracy in her writing. A record (for *The Golden Age*) of deep reading of Jewish authors including the canonical works of György Konrád, Paul Celan, Imre Kertész and Maurice Blanchot as well as memoirs by Kitty Sandy, Teri Korda and Lenke Arnstein, which tell of Budapest war experiences and later lives in Australia, sits alongside queries about heating in Budapest apartments during the Second World War.[26] When writing the novel that would become *Gilgamesh* and therefore thinking about Edith and Jim's journey from the south-west of Western Australia to Armenia, London directs herself to 'Write to Head Office, Director of Passports', presumably to ask about 'Age child of own passport; small child on mother's passport.'[27] To cement this duty to realism, in notes London made as part of an intended talk about *Gilgamesh* on its publication, she relates how her characters' journey

> became my journey; a journey of research. I had to work out how much money she would need—what a fare on a cargo boat from Australia to England would cost, and a third-class fare on the Orient Express to Istanbul. I had to work out how she would get this money. Above all I had to find a way in which she could get into the Soviet Union without a visa, and be allowed to stay there for some years. I had to make her journey feasible.[28]

If London wondered at how to give her character access to the Soviet Union, then she herself was given imaginative admittance by another of her major influences: the writings of nineteenth-century Russian authors, who London justifiably speaks of as 'giants', and in particular Chekhov.[29] It is no coincidence that one of the parent characters in *The Good Parents* reads Leo Tolstoy; his estranged daughter has by her bed an unread copy of Chekhov's short stories gifted to her by her father. After all, while Chekhov is counted among the greats of Russian literature, he made his writing of short stories a point of generational difference from the epic novelists of the earlier nineteenth century, including Tolstoy. London tells of her admiration of Chekhov's narratives, of 'how he writes of familiar situations, of small things that happen all the time to all if us, which subtly affect us, in the constant teeming moments of our lives'.[30] And most resonant for the concerns of her own writing and what she brings to Australian literature, is London's perceptive sense that Chekhov's stories turn on those 'moments when we change'.[31] As with Chekhov's work, such unexpected moments of quiet transformation, as often barely perceptible as profoundly felt, constantly interest London's writing.

Each of the chapters that follows attends to this persistent preoccupation with change, and introduces and engages with the short story volumes and novels in turn, and in order of their publication. This is an approach called for by the writing itself: looking across London's volumes, it becomes apparent very quickly that while there are some shared ideas threading through her body of work, each text—even within a particular volume, as with the short stories—houses its own concerns, both thematic and stylistic. Because London has not been as prolific or as public as many of her contemporaries, an assumption (an erroneous one, perhaps) has been made here that London's earlier short stories may be less familiar to today's readers than the novels. On that basis, the first chapter, which addresses the two short story collections, aims to tell of the exploration the stories undertake of their form and their diverse thematic preoccupations. The chapters on each of the three novels offer closer readings to illuminate their specific interests and to draw from these London's singular contributions to Australian literature.

The Short Stories: *Sister Ships* and *Letter to Constantine*

Joan London's literary career started with the short story. Prior to the publication of two collections with Fremantle Arts Centre Press, London was writing occasional stories for local literary journals such as *Westerly Magazine* and edited volumes with helpfully self-explanatory titles including *Decade: A Selection of Contemporary Western Australian Short Fiction* (1982). As is so often the case with short story publication patterns and the curation of short story volumes, these stories, already published in other outlets, came to form part of *Sister Ships* (1986).[1] Ray Coffey, Fremantle Arts Centre Press editor, was full of praise for London's first book, telling her that 'this will be a strong collection'.[2] *Letter to Constantine* (1993) followed and featured stories that, like those appearing in *Sister Ships*, had enjoyed local publication.[3] But unlike the earlier volume, London's second collection featured narratives that had also found audiences further afield. 'The Angry Girl', for example, was published under the Bloomsbury (United Kingdom) imprint as part of a collection edited by a New Zealand poet and short story writer. And 'Letter to Constantine', which would lend the second collection its title and serve as its opening story, appeared in the volume *Millennium: Time-Pieces by Australian Writers* (1991), a subtitle that suggests London's growing national literary presence. However, her stories roam beyond national borders and refuse character types. Moreover, such a neat narrative of career progression, which suggests a stepping out from the literary regions to the national big stage, only tells a (distorted) part of London's short-story career trajectory. In 1986 *Sister Ships* was also released in the United States by the multinational book publisher Viking Penguin; when *Letter to Constantine* was published, London's American agent was unable to place the book, citing a decisive turn away from the short story form in the North American literary market. London has herself reflected on how her two short-story volumes spring both from her pen and wider circumstances:

> My first book, which largely drew, as so many first books do, on my own experience, was written during a flowing of women's writing worldwide as a result of the women's movement ... —in Australia I think of Elizabeth Jolley, Helen Garner, Kate Grenville—and created a whole new audience and reception for writing by women. This wasn't the reason I wrote, but it was an encouraging climate in which to begin to publish.
>
> My second book was written across the years in which a lot of fiction was emerging from the influence of Literary Theory, a time of exceptional experimentation with the short story form, of fragmentation, ficto-criticism, meta-fiction, minimalism—writing that draws attention to itself as writing—and while these theoretical issues had little currency for me—I was told by a friend who was compiling a postmodern anthology that my writing couldn't be included

> because my commitment to narrative was old-fashioned—I think it encouraged me to be more daring in the narrative shape of the stories.[4]

London's comments suggest a commitment to her own art; one that is aware of the social and literary contexts that variously support and accord value to certain forms of writing but nevertheless chooses to go its own way. And as to why London wrote short stories at all, she says simply, 'that was the form in which my inspiration came to me', until it didn't.[5] And she takes pleasure in the challenges the short story form presents to readers, as well as writers:

> It can be harder, I think, to read a collection of short stories than a longer form. So many beginnings and endings. One life after another at its moment of intensity. So many little worlds set up which then have to justify their own meaning and sense of closure. Not subject to an overriding narrative project, the short story arises from a very direct response to experience. Its intensity can only be sustained by feeling. Above all it cannot afford complacency, staleness or the blunting of feeling.[6]

With their concentrated worlds that surprise and purposefully puzzle, London's short stories are carried by their explorations of character, sensation and the compressed narrative form itself.

Sister Ships

London did not set out to call her first short story collection *Sister Ships*. It was a title she ended up taking from the last story she wrote for the book and which became the volume's opening piece. As she told of this origin tale to the 1987 Warana Writers' Week Brisbane audience, gathered to hear a then-emerging writer from Fremantle in Western Australia:

> For a while, I was going to call it 'Enough Rope', though I wasn't very happy with that, especially when I discovered that Dorothy Parker had written a volume of poetry called that in the thirties, and that a B-grade movie of the same name had recently been made. But then I came to that title finally, as I was writing the story, I knew that was what I wanted to call the book, that I had been writing about the lives of women, passing by one another, going their own way.[7]

At the time, London was thirty-eight years old and a writer to watch. *Sister Ships* had won the 1986 *The Age* Book of the Year award, having been completed with the assistance of a $17,000 New Writers' Fellowship from the Literature Board of the Australia Council. The collection was also the recipient of a Western Australian Arts Council Literary Prize, nudging out from the top spot *That Eye The Sky* (1986) by an author who has come to personify 'Western Australian writing': Tim Winton.[8] London herself was being celebrated—the distinguished poet and editor, Judith Rodriguez, correctly foretold that London was 'destined for the top rank of story writing'[9]—and as her presence at the Warana Writers' Week attested, invitations to literary events were increasing as an indication of her rising reputation. By 2005, and with Martu woman and author Nugi Garimara (Doris Pilkington), London would be the drawcard of the Asialink Author tour of Singapore and China, designed to raise the international profile of Australian writing and to promote economic and cultural ties between Asia and Australia. And it was an admiration that would continue as London's literary career unfolded at its unhurried pace. But as she was explaining to her new readers in 1987, she was foremost a writer with good instincts. London's concern to 'get right' the title of a first book is completely understandable for any author; the title at which London arrived—with its sense of drift and hoped-for destination, and emphasis on female experiences—captures the volume's preoccupations. And as she told another audience in September 1993: 'It's hard to define your own work, but I would say that *Sister Ships* is a book about finding where you stand'.[10] The title also highlights many of the themes on which her later writing would turn.

Eight short stories comprise the volume and there is evidence across these stories of London experimenting with voice and point of view, not just as a new writer trying out the narrative tools at her disposal, but also to represent a variety of (white) women's experiences at a particular historical moment. London expressly identified her emphasis on this specific time in an interview she gave to *Fremantle Arts Review* on *Sister Ships'* publication. She remarked:

> Women went through a time of great change. A lot of the pressures that had been social and came from family, or from society in general—to be nice, to be good, to be affectionate, to be passive and not to displease anyone ... I think feminism has gone very deep into our perception of life. I don't know of any woman, or any man, who has not been influenced by the movements of the 1960s and 1970s. It affirmed for me the importance of doing what I really

> wanted to do (that's a human need, not just a female one), although I am not a card-carrying feminist.[11]

There is some hint at what being a 'card-carrying feminist' might entail for London later in the interview when she refers to her writerly interest in women 'beyond the political movements of feminism and its extremes'.[12] It is only speculation, but London could have had in mind the strident terms with which the poet Kate Jennings, London's contemporary, concluded her Vietnam War moratorium rally speech at Sydney University in 1970 and which set the passionate tones of protest that marked the decades to come:

> and i say to every woman that every time you're put down or fucked over, every time they kick you cunningly in the teeth, go stand on the street corner and tell every man that walks by, every one of them a male chauvinist by virtue of **HIS** birthright, tell them all to go suck their own cocks. and when they laugh, tell them that they're getting bloody defensive, and that you know what size weapon to buy to kill the bodies that unfortunately you've laid under often enough.
>
> **ALL POWER TO WOMEN.**[13]

This register is certainly not London's, which may have put her at odds with some of her peers and those readers seeking a particular kind of feminist empowerment in Australian literature. But it is didacticism and dogma that London wants to avoid in her writing, and so very early on sets herself the challenge of representing in small scale wider social issues taking place in Australia and beyond, without turning her writing into a manifesto. London holds onto the imaginative possibilities of narrative and resists the possible narrowing effects of certainty, whether political or personal. This concern is underscored when she told her interviewer that 'I'm not just wanting to write about my own experiences', although these did play a part in her short stories (and later novels) as London later related when she spoke of her writerly beginnings at the 2004 Sydney Writers' Festival:[14]

> When I wrote my first book, I didn't have much time, small children, study, part-time job, but I don't think that's why I wrote stories. All of a sudden, incidents from my past seemed to present themselves, ripe for exploration, each separate and significant in a way that it hadn't seemed at the time. A trip on an ocean liner, sharing a house with incompatible people, trying to live in the country, travelling overland through Asia, something my mother once said.[15]

London's first collection of short stories specialises in these quotidian situations. The collection as whole, like each of its constituent stories in its own way, takes a studied interest in women and girls as they negotiate relationships with friends, family, intimates. And the commonality of the stories is the sense that they are of, and represent, a time of change, whether that be a coming of age, generational shifts or novel sexual liberation, which has enfolded within it specifically gendered experiences.

The story 'Travelling' is one example. In this narrative, a newlywed woman is on the hippie trail, unhappy and doubting. That she is on this route speaks to the subculture of alternative travel and experience that signified the hopes, and fantasies, of a famed, and mythologised, generation (which elsewhere in London's writing, especially *The Good Parents* (2008), is further reflected on and gently critiqued). Ruth and her husband, Galen, have been thrown together with two other self-styled international adventurers, Bob and Canada, with the group pictured moving through the streets of Luang Prabang 'like an awkward beast whose legs wished to go different ways' (83), half-aware of the Laotian Civil War being fought around them and mostly thoughtless of their privilege, which London makes explicit to the reader. Contrary to the intended orientating purpose of the '*Student's Guide to South-East Asia*' the characters consult—a guidebook that carries echoes of the early blockbuster Lonely Planet title, *South-East Asia on a Shoestring* (1975) which was, for a certain generation, as much a guide to cheap accommodation as to a lifestyle—Ruth is adrift. As London writes:

> She felt she'd lost a whole persona somewhere along the trail. Become a mere trudging mate whom nobody seemed to hear. It wasn't just that mascara streaked down your face in the humidity and long hair was out of the question, you just tucked it back as best you could. She hated to catch sight of herself in shop mirrors. A large girl with a bare earnest face. Sexless as a missionary. And fat. Getting fatter. There were no shadows, no roles, no corners to hide in anywhere. Just the fact of yourself coming to meet you border after border. (77–8)

Ruth's confrontation with herself is imagined in part by the movement not only of travel but also by the subtle shift London enacts between her character's inner and external lives. And it is further rendered in explicitly gendered terms that are thrown into sharp relief by a flippant but meaningful remark made immediately following Ruth's ruminations: '"The women in these parts are supposed to be the most beautiful in the world",

Canada said to Galen' (78). Ruth feels herself both invisible and exposed, shadowed by the casual sexism volleyed between the male characters who presume a capacity, in the world of this short story, to 'fit together the puzzle of map and reality' (83) and who are untroubled by their gender. By contrast, Ruth is given to feeling greatly her femaleness, just as much as *Sister Ships* more broadly is devoted to representing and querying across and between its constituent stories such gendered circumstances.

Therefore, and as befits the short-story form, London's stories in *Sister Ships* are character-focused rather than plot-driven. Plot, a contrivance designed to organise events and knowledge, is something to which the young playwright, Jonelle Hughes, in 'First Night'—the second of the short stories in the collection—is particularly attuned as she remarks at one point: 'What was going to happen next? Something had to happen' (40). And yet, it is a convention she comes to quietly question, much as the short story in which she appears does. Jonelle intuits that all-too-familiar storylines—'The incinerator *ghostly in the moonlight. "The homeless girl shivered ..."*'—are giving way to those '[r]eal things [that] were at last happening to her' (42) and which might not be easily known or represented. These intuited 'real things' are not developed as a plot point in London's story. Instead, they are associatively yoked with the darkened backyard that occasions the story's concluding image of the suburban sublime: 'the sprinkler rearing in the middle of the lawn, the silver pyramid of the Hills Hoist, the two bins sentried at the back steps, gleamed with their own taut power' (42). If the story does have a plot point at all, it is enmeshed in the domestic power dynamics in the background that see the mother of Antonia De Witt, Jonelle's neighbour, come to agree reluctantly that the girls can use the family dining table for their theatrical requirements 'if we keep it covered with a rug' (38). Thanks to the intercession of the overly affable and unfaithful Mr De Witt, the young girls' planned performance, threatened with cancellation, can be enacted after all. But this outcome offers no resolution to the adult relationships that play out around the half-comprehending girls.

To say that 'First Night' is about a group of young girls who put on a show of *Cinderella* for their parents is a fair summary of the story's narrative. But it is a poor approximation of both London's deft telling of the lives of families whose proximity as neighbours only highlights their differences, and the story's centring on girls with their own worries and preoccupations, who encounter the adult world. Jonelle remembers and internalises her family's injunction—'Don't show off' (39)—which echoes across the page of London's story as the girls imagine, and act out, Cinderella's experience of stepmotherly constraint: '*Cinderella! What is the meaning of this? / When I kindly took you under my wing, I did not mean for you to dance and sing / All day*' (38). Similarly, when Antonia tells Jonelle that 'I will never have children … It spoils the figure' (36), the implication London is asking her readers to recognise is that her young female character is unthinkingly rehearsing not her own desires but what she has heard from adult women.

The girls' role-playing both on and off the stage in 'First Night' suggests the concern that London's collection has in examining the parts women enact in their everyday lives. In the same interview with *Fremantle Arts Review* London gave on the release of *Sister Ships*, she highlights this preoccupation, singling out the short story 'New Year', which sees new parents, Rowena and Harry, living with a new-born baby and another young couple, Diane and 'Hutch' Hutchison, who own the house they uneasily share. In retrospect, this story, with its multiple characters, anticipates the preference for ensemble scenarios that will later distinguish London's novels. But at its moment of publication London noted:

> The expectations and the traditional training for that role [motherhood] can be stifling, not only for the mother, but also for the father who is facing other new challenges and pressures. In my story 'New Year', Rowena is trying to reconcile following her own life with the role of motherhood. The two are not very compatible. Rowena is completely bowled over by the experience of her first child and is cut off, as I think anybody with a new baby is cut off. It makes complete demands on a woman, and she has to totally give herself up to it. In this story, this is not accepted by the people she is living with, and she finds herself trying to respond to what is required of her, to the ethos of the house in which she lives.[16]

The scene for this short story, a hot New Year's Eve told in the immediacy of the present tense and focalised through Rowena's third person point of view, certainly entertains these tensions, centring on the demands made on Rowena by a feeding baby and what the other adults around her claim as enlightened views. For a story set on the eve of a new year, a magnified moment in and of time, the characters give little attention to the future or indeed the past, with Rowena being the exception. The present tense in which the story is composed underlines the characters' commitment to living in and for the moment, a marker of what they see as their progressive lifestyles, with Rowena providing a telling point of contrast.

Rowena represents in this story a model of femininity that is out of time. Her husband and housemates sit around casually with their celebratory wine and hint repeatedly at their desires, or at least the image of sexual freedom they have of themselves: 'we're a hedonist culture. On a night like this we ought to take off the lot' (44). In deliberate comparison, Rowena is often elsewhere in the house, tending to her infant, Tom; recalling a recent life with Harry and their child in a rudimentary beach shack; and feeling the judgement of the others: 'Lately Rowena has suspected a consensus in the house about her, about maternal over-commitment' (44). She is not wrong. Hutch takes the opportunity during the evening to remark superciliously: '"The Madonna", Hutch says. "I take it that's what you want to be"' (48). Diane, too, voices incredulity: '"How do you bear it? … Why do people *do* this to themselves d'you think?"' (48, 49). And Harry is remembered by Rowena as projecting onto her drunken anxieties and frustrated longings while nursing their child: '"Do something different!" … "Is this all you ever do? Surprise me! Surprise me sometimes why don't you"' (51). Focused on their present and its imagined freedoms, the other characters treat Rowena with some disdain. Yet, it is from this tangle of memory and present pressures the short story's conclusion returns Rowena to an uncertain celebratory pleasure in her own body that has the effect of also questioning such judgements.

The act of preparing a fruit salad alone, wine fizzing and music throbbing, sees the narrative shift from the dialogue that characterises the evening and the short story itself towards a tumbling, crescendo-like stream of consciousness, which captures what can be interpreted as Rowena's momentary psychological and physical release:

> The big knife has made her bold, slicing through cheeks of pink flesh … it comes away from the rinds with a sucking sound … take it all off … Rowena chops, she is hot, she has never felt so hot … It is so simple. It works with the speed of a good idea. To unbuckle. Unpeel. To step out of the overalls, kick at them, and feel that trusty roughness, thigh against thigh. She gathers up the rinds, pips, peel, and dumps them in the sink. Why stop there? Already she is moving easily, the T-shirt slips easily up her spine, cooling it, releasing her head. … Her breasts come loping out of their milk-stiffened cups, she could almost fear for them as she bends over her knife … the final touches … pants, you need two hands and they're over your knees, binding them, but—you just step out of them … She's wading in her own clothes, hands plunged up to the wrists in fruit, mixing it, the passionfruit sprays out as she squeezes its upturned pouch … She washes her hands. (53)

The colours London evokes in this scene—'pink, all shades of pink, orange, tawny' (53) bring a painterly aspect; the present tense defies any fixing of this image as a still life. And with its patterned alliteration and rolling rhythm, the passage is sensual in a way that echoes, but is not immediately of the order of, the heterosexual hedonism which the other characters flirtatiously, but laboriously, refer to all evening.

London makes this disjunct clear when, on the symbolic strike of midnight, she has Rowena carry herself and the bowl to the others, as though in Marcel Duchamp painting or partaking in a solemn procession of offering: 'Here is Rowena, descending a staircase, her bowl held before her … She is only aware of the whiteness beneath her, this company of globes and triangles, trusting them with her own grave progress' (53).

It is a diptych image, too, hinged punningly and meaningfully: earlier in the story, Rowena is imagined moving down the stairs, listening for her child, and feeling 'a fruitless swinging to her arms, she is breasting dark air' (44). Given the artfulness of the passages that precede it, the description of Rowena's reception is jarring: 'And the faces looking up at her are frozen, their mouths are frozen open as if they cannot open wide enough for their laughter, they are stamping their feet, clutching their chairs with laugher' (53). The tone here is of the burlesque, with the repetition of 'their' emphasising a stark division between Rowena and the others who misread her appearance as an assent to their hitherto unrealised sexual ménage: 'Something white flies by and catches on the vines. Clothing? Actions bring results …' (54). But London has Rowena deny this fantasy cliché.

Offering a reply of sorts to her husband's remembered want of her to do something unexpected, the story ends with Rowena placing the fruit before him and saying, 'Here you are' (54) but not before a private acknowledgement that carries layered meanings: '… but she is beginning to feel a drop, a fatal fading of interest. She has already been delivered of one miracle. She is tired' (54). This notion of a sent wonder recalls an earlier, secular image of Tom, 'at night the neighbours' bathroom light beacons through the louvres and … the roundness of Tom's head, is outlined in this dull radiance' (46) and also suggests both Rowena's contrary feelings towards the birth of her child and the fleeting freedom and exclusive intensity of that fleshly, sensory moment at the stroke of midnight. There is no resolution. With this story, London is doing much more than describing characters and their situations; something is also being said about the difficulties and pleasures of motherhood and female experience at a time when both are being socially and politically reimagined.

'New Year' also points to an interest of the short story form itself that finds expression across many of the narratives in *Sister Ships* insofar as the volume's characters are consistently confined together in small spaces. Throughout the collection, London places her characters in enclosed settings to shape the interactions the stories observe. Rowena and Harry share a house with the Hutchisons; they sleep on a mattress, '[t]heir room is another piece of the verandah, a partitioned cavern' (45–6), with the temporary nature of their claims contributing to the uncertainty Rowena feels. In 'Travelling', the Laotian capital Luang Prabang is infiltrated by the CIA but more immediately for the main characters, they live (too) closely and provisionally; memorably, Ruth listens at night to 'Bob's horny feet manipulating plastic of his sleeping bag, positioned close by (80). In the rooms of a house with jazz playing and the rain beating steadily, Michael and the first-person female narrator of the would-be titular story, 'Enough Rope', circle each other emotionally and physically, their relationship uncertain but long-standing. And 'Burning Off', the concluding story of the collection, returns to the configuration of 'New Year' and sees two young couples, one with a baby, spending some time together on a verandah in a non-descript bush town. It is also one story about which London had much earlier ideas, and it has autobiographical origins. In a prose poem precisely dated 'November 11th, 1975', London wrote:

> It's nearly summer in York.
> I found the sheen of the long yellow grass
> around the cottage, down to the creek
> beautiful
> …

Dreamily I cared for my child, her first year nearly over.
Then casually the council men set fire to the grass.
Here, here, here the fire roars
...
Outside is blackened, charred, reduced to earth.
The smoke hangs on, all poetry is gone.
Ready for summer.[17]

The characters in 'Burning Off' emerge from this poem; they are forging a life they think of as different from their parents and which is scorned by their neighbour, a stand-in for the imagined attitudes of earlier generations: 'your university types, your bra-burners, unionists and what have you' (108). The announcement of the dismissal of Gough Whitlam's progressive Labor government at the close of both the story and the volume (and indeed at the end of that earlier poem written on the day of the constitutional crisis) raises unanswered questions about the social and personal headway the characters believe they have made. The unnamed first-person female narrator comes to wonder at how different their generation really is from that of their parents; one of the husbands half-jokingly advises the women to '[h]ave a sewing circle' (115) while he works as a manual labourer. These are gendered arrangements that suggests their political ideals represented in the story by 'Indian gods behind the kitchen door. Over the stove, a newspaper cutting of Whitlam and Barnard waving after they had announced the conscription amnesty' (110–1) have not been realised.

These stories—'New Year', 'Travelling' and 'Burning Off'—involve young heterosexual couples, and particularly attend to the women of these pairings, but London widens her reach in the volume to focus on women of various ages, some in similarly constrained conditions both physically and existentially. 'Sister Ships', the volume's first story, takes place, as the title infers, on a boat; a floating social microcosm with a long literary heritage which, as London's story remembers, is bound up with the projects and legacies of empire. This narrative is trained on Hull, a young woman known appropriately enough by her nautical nickname, who is just out of high-school and tracing an earlier journey her parents made from Perth in Western Australia to England. Her travel is presented as an obligatory rite of passage, a coming-of-age story, and from the opening pages it is apparent that London is having some (serious) fun with the scenario she is presenting to her readers.

Within the space of the ship, Hull finds herself in various states of close company with humorous effect. Hull shares a cabin with two other young women: the pink shirt she purchased with her mother in preparation for chaste 'deck games' (10) is quickly commandeered by one of them who has other interests in mind and prompts Hull to part-work her way through the ideas of feminine propriety she carries: 'do you think she looks *hard*? Do you think she looks older than seventeen? I think swearing is unfeminine. Does she swear in front of men? What is sex-appeal anyway? She's got a lot of nice clothes herself, I don't know why she…' (12). Dramatic irony abounds, and the ship's dining room is another space that affords Hull encounters with haphazard company that seems to mean more than Hull knows: a mysterious German man who possibly—it is left uncertain as Hull experiences drunken hallucinations—seduces or violates the teenager at the story's end; a young man interested in Hull's cabin-mate; and a slightly older woman, Marie, who readily partakes in the waggishly named 'Fried Schnapper à la Saint-Germaine' and 'Bon Fillet à l'Anglaise with Ribbon Potatoes', and purloins the dinner rolls because 'Nan and I get starving after Bingo' (19). The characters in London's story bounce off each other, even when avoidance is at times their objective as the constrained space of the ship, and of the short story form itself, means that they cannot help but be in each other's range.

The story culminates, as does the journey, with the Grand Parade—'the farewell do' (23) – and London's wit is on full display. Hull finds herself wrapped in crepe paper and crowned with a cylinder: '"Sister Ships," says Marie. "These are our Funnels. Aren't I clever? ... The idea is, in the Grand Parade we sort of run past each other blowing our whistles"' (23). A reader might be amused, or aghast, at the thought; Hull is tellingly compliant. The two women attend the parade, arrive late, and so miss the opportunity to showcase their outfits. 'Dennis from Bingo', with whom Hull clammily dances, wonders aloud if they are 'Nurses? The Ku Klux Klan?' (24), thus entirely missing the costume's unlikely significance for both Hull and London's short story collection. While there is certainly a sense of the ridiculous attached to the fancy dress scenario, it also recalls an earlier moment in the story that saw Hull notice the passing at sea of a sister ship and so drew attention to the collection's interest in the parallel lives of women. As London details in the interview in which she discusses the volume and makes mention of this story:

> The vision of the sistership, that she [Hull] actually sees passing their own ship at sea, and the various women she is travelling with, who lead lives of their own, yet from whom she is also learning, opens up the whole idea of parallel lives.

> The girl realises that she is ultimately alone, as the ship is alone, taking its own course.[18]

The collective of women the volume curates shifts between this idea of women being alone and as living co-existences. 'Lilies', a story that appears in the second half of the collection and is one of the earliest that London wrote—it was first published in 1982 in an anthology—especially enacts this dual movement. It starts with a thirty-something daughter and her mother momentarily coming to live together after some years apart. From its beginning, the story seems as though it will centre on Christine Hollins, the daughter, but as it unfolds the main character becomes her mother, Violet, who unlike most of London's characters spends extended narrative time outside rather than in enclosed spaces, her daughters always present in mind. She thinks to herself: 'My daughters are strangers to me. She sometimes said that to herself to try to work it out. Because this couldn't be the whole story, the way they looked at her sometimes with hard grown-up faces that made her nervous' (93). But what is most apparent is the revelation of parts of her own 'whole story' that are perhaps unexpected for a wife of a parish priest and of which her daughter has no idea. Surfacing in long passages of internal monologue is a remembered affair she had; the shame of realising she was but one example of a man's unfaithful habit; and its unspokenness that has nevertheless been etched in 'the patterns rutted across their [her children's] souls' (106). This story is the most ruminative of the collection, in keeping with an older woman with a long life shown to intersect in mysterious ways with the experiences of her child.

Generational relationships between mothers and daughters are also of interest to the story, 'The Girls Love Each Other', which, in line with London's experimentation in point of view and tense in the volume, is written in the first-person, from the past perspective of Jan Jones. Jan is a down-to-earth hairdresser and a mother to Morveen, who is on the cusp of adulthood. In the story, Jan and her friend Beth represent an older generation of women; alongside them, Morveen and her friends, who come to stay with Jan, are presented in the story as beginning to make their own claims on the world. Morveen has plans to move from Perth to Sydney to live with '[s]ix girls' (63). There are 'no boyfriends' in sight (55), so the implication that Jan half-discerns is that her daughter's future and desires are distinct from her own heterosexual entanglements. Yet, insofar as these differences with Morveen are established, Jan also acknowledges the importance of her friendship with Beth. She recognises that her independence is founded on the two women's supportive interdependence: 'she taught me: you always pay your own way' (62).

Hence London's attributing to Beth the story's future-looking last words is meaningful. Much of the narrative is focused on the near-present; the patterning of similar phrases such as 'last week' (55) and 'last Saturday' (59) and 'Friday is our busy day at the salon' (57) gives a sense of the everyday that Jan and Beth inhabit. But unlike 'New Year', which has Rowena caught in time, this story imagines imminent prospects for its female characters. As Jan hesitates over a decision to follow Morveen to Sydney by invitation and for a holiday, Beth turns to the future: '"Well, hang it all", Beth said out of the silence. "Hang it all, why don't you go?"' (64). This gesture is the short story's concluding note and it draws the mother and daughter into a relationship of imaginative proximity and possibility, towards which the collection itself, with its parallel lives of women, is ultimately turned.

Letter to Constantine

Speaking with the author Gail Jones on the publication of her second short story collection, *Letter to Constantine* (1993)—Jones' own first volume of short stories, *The House of Breathing* (1992), had been released by the same publisher a year before[19]—London shared her approach to writing: 'Before I begin a story I have to see a picture in my head, and then, and then, and then. I have a single image I'm working towards, and I'm trying to do justice to that image, to have earned that image, to justify it.'[20] This idea of a concentrated image, as both inspiration and terminus, is one that London returns to in her later novels—*The Good Parents*, for one, is expressly indebted to cinema—and it finds full expression in *Letter to Constantine*, which reads largely as though a dream. It is not only that many of London's characters in these eight short stories are caught dreaming. The free association of unconscious thinking that dreams are made of is resonant with the stories' thematic and stylistic preoccupations, marking a significant shift from the formal interests of *Sister Ships* and that volume's centring of the everyday lives of women.

London herself commented on this change in a talk on the short story form she gave in Melbourne in 1992, when she was writing what would become the last story of the *Letter to Constantine* collection, 'Maisie Goes to India'. Modestly declaring herself a novice in the art of the short story, London told the audience of her writing process:

> When I finished my first collection of stories I knew I wanted to change. I did not know how, or in which direction. It was not an intellectual decision. It was, if anything,

> visceral: I felt as if I wanted to stretch, I wanted more room to breathe. For a long time I did not write anything at all.
>
> I knew by then that a collection of stories (and I tend to think in terms of collection, rather than individual publication), like any book, represents a collection of thoughts and images that have preoccupied a writer across a certain period of time.
>
> ...
>
> It wasn't until I came upon an old dream jotted down in a notebook, a dream from which previous, personal connotations had faded, leaving only the stark outlines of its landscape and the tracks of feeling that it contained, that I started to move in the direction I wanted to go. In writing the story that arose from this dream [the first, titular story] I discovered I could move in space and time, anywhere that existed in my imagination, and that in the lift and stretch of the imagination to create this landscape, I was released into a larger world. This landscape was the closest representation of my feelings and thoughts at that time.[21]

London would also find unexpected inspiration in a dream for her next book and first novel, *Gilgamesh* (2001), which is grounded in far more recognisable history and place than a *Letter to Constantine*, with its oftentimes surreal settings and dream-focused characters. 'Pinch Me, Pinch Me', one story in the *Letter to Constantine* volume, begins with the relating of one sister's dream of another. The first line of 'The Inlet', a later story in the collection, conjures images that surface in the dark: 'Nights at the inlet were long and black and filled with strenuous dreams' (78). And the same narrative, which is otherwise a story of childhood holidaying and the mischiefs and family fissures it involves, ends with a wretched vision of what remains when two of four tourist friends are swept out to sea: 'We watched them stumble, and keep walking, against the wind, looking straight head. Walking and walking as you do in a dream, as if part of you wasn't there any more, as if part of you too had drowned' (87). The reality of shock and grief calls on the dissociation of dreams.

In a very different mode, another story in the collection titled 'The Second Stage', which begins where Marc Chagall's autobiography, *My Life* (1923), finishes (with Chagall at the age of thirty-five), has the artist's unrecorded life take on dreamy distortions: 'Last night he dreamt he was alone, spotlit, on the stage of the Ballets Russes. He'd been given as a costume a crumpled peasant smock. Disdainful faces—Bakst? Diaghilev?—were watching from the wings. He could hear that audience's murmur, waiting for him to begin' (102). 'Angels', the collection's second story, commences with its male figure shifting between sleep and wakefulness, and what he envisions—'Snowbirds ... They seemed like a new species come to a new world' (28)—is both phantasmic and certain. And the volume opens on a hypnopompic register, with the first-person narrator of the titular story introducing in the present tense an address to the absent Constantine: 'Your presence was natural to me as a dream is on first waking' (11). In the story titled 'The Woman Who Only Answered Yes or No', the idea to make a film of Anton Chekhov's play *The Seagull* comes when Steiner, a director, is asleep. And the telling of this vision by his scriptwriter-lover who narrates the story in first-person is worth quoting at some length as it points to shared qualities of cinema and dreaming in which the story itself takes a studied interest:[22]

> You won't find this mentioned in any interview: producers are not known for backing dreams. But he told me about it a few nights later. In this dream, he said, he was flying, across a mighty stretch of water that gleamed silver against distant plains. Closer, and he made out mountains and fields and rivers branching into marshland and patchy beaches amongst banks of reeds. On the shore was a lone building, a wooden inn or country house, its windows shining silver like water. This seemed to be his destination. Tiny figures on a balcony were running up and down, pointing past him, to the clouds. He looked up. Out of the clouds huge black curving shapes were hurtling straight towards him. He swerved and saw they were not birds or stars but letters. He recognised the Cyrillic alphabet. These are the titles, Steiner thought, and I am reading them. He woke with the words *The Seagull* in his head.
>
> Straight away he'd stumbled out of bed and found Chekhov's play and opened it at random and read: *We should show life neither as it is nor as it ought to be but as we see it in our dreams.* Treplev's speech. (43)

Konstantin Treplev's unhappy ending notwithstanding—this author takes his own life offstage in the play's conclusion—the speech encountered all too serendipitously in wakefulness by Steiner announces the tone of the short story in which it is related. It also makes the narrative's presiding claim that dreams and cinema might have much in common.

Beyond any one individual story, *Letter to Constantine* throughout offers to its readers a kind of dream knowledge that emerges from the depiction of seemingly two contradictory states—reverie and reality—and which is also an effect of the stories' elliptical qualities. The stories that comprise *Letter to Constantine* are not straightforward in their telling; they are marked by juxtapositions of image and time, and invite imaginative engagement and emotional response. Given the account she offers of her own writing practice, it is perhaps meaningful that London has in 'The Woman Who Only Answered Yes or No' a female scriptwriter, similarly working to realise an image—in this instance of a woman descending a hill—speak what might be thought of as the collection's logic: 'Did I hope to uncover a mystery? We worked by suggestion, hunches, clues. One image led to another, seemed to find an answering echo within me' (57). What London's stories in this volume leave their reader with is an impression rather than a solution. The narratives of which *Letter to Constantine* consists, both individually and together, are interested in that which is intuited and felt, and which promises to evade easy approximation in language.

The stories are therefore difficult to summarise; they certainly do not hold themselves out to be put in the service of 'big national stories or iconic landscapes'. If what holds them together is their oneiric or dream-like properties, then it is because, as Gail Jones points out in her interview with London: 'they are disposed nomadically through various times and spaces, range from Russia, to England, to France, to India, to Western Australia; they globe-trot, boundary ride, migrate and emigrate'.[23] For all their shared dream interests, each story in this collection is resolutely different from the next and refuses to sit still.

The final story, 'Maisie Goes to India', for example, is dedicated to London's parents and was understood by London at the time of its writing to mark a return 'to all that is most familiar to me, to material that is so well known to me it is proving hard to see. It's the story many writers come to write at some time, in some form, the story of their parents ... Perhaps a story like this is a sort of farewell'.[24] It is an envisaged voyage that London's mother took from Fremantle to Imperial India as a young woman. The first-person narrator wonders at her presumption, and desire, to relate and know her mother's life, acknowledging that 'I don't want to be nostalgic about this' (122). One way of addressing what is presented as risky romanticism is to time-travel; to become an otherwise impossible witness to her parents' youthful parting at the berth, which is presented in non-sentimental terms: 'On the deck a young woman has just stopped waving. On the quay a young man lets his crumpled streamer fall to his feet' (122). Yet if reminiscence is shunned, imaginative transportation is privileged in the story as a gift of inheritance and a form of creative remembrance: '*It's your story now. I've forgotten*' (141).

In other stories, it is as though imagination itself is the subject, constituting the narrative landscape. The collection's first story, 'Letter to Constantine', sees a former art historian, Magda, ruminate on a past that carries simultaneously a sense of timelessness and a temporal cleft marked by a before and an after, with some seeming economic catastrophe the turning point. ('After' there is no need for historians of the visual, with the narrator instead taking on the job of punching numbers into a computer to determine access to rationed food. Musicians, in contrast, are essential workers). Distinct from a later story in the collection, 'The Inlet', which is narrated from a young girl's point of view and is secured in time as well as place—references are made, for example, to the south-west town of Albany in Western Australia and a summer childhood of caravan parks, games and jellyfish—'Letter to Constantine' moves between the desert and the sea, which are less geographic locations than mythopoetic spaces.[25] The story itself comes to look like an answer to Constantine's gentle injunction to the narrator, which serves as its conclusion: '"The world is of your own making," you said, ... "Write," you said' (27). As the introductory piece to the collection, 'Letter to Constantine' announces both the volume's inventive disorientation and the undertaking it makes to its readers, namely that 'larger patterns promised to emerge' (19). The reader has been advised, though; this surfacing will be redolent rather than readily recognisable.

In some stories in *Letter to Constantine*, characters are pictured as implicitly impatient with the volume's dream logic. In 'The Woman Who Only Answered Yes or No', Jacob, an assistant cameraman, articulates his irritation at what he sees as the unorthodox approach to film-making his scriptwriter companion (and perhaps London as author) is taking in her pursuit of her film titled '*The Woman*' (43): '"This piecemeal way we do things," he said, "where will it end?"' (58). The scriptwriter's unsaid response is telling:

> I had no answer. All that I had were some images of a woman's life, on unprinted reels, images I had not even seen. The archival footage of the civil war in her country, the sequence of the young woman in the fur coat hurrying down a bombed-out street, the troupe of travelling players fleeing with their tent, all this came later, existed then only as ideas in my head. I did not yet know what the film's truth was, the images' linking

> thread. Each image we filmed seemed to end in silence. I only knew my destination was my image of the women on the hill. In the end, I told myself, silence will speak. (58)

This placing together of images, some found, some uncertain, is how the story (and the collection) is patterned. But, as it happens, the destination of '*The Woman*' is not as the scriptwriter had imagined her film. The visual aspect she arrives at is not of a woman descending a hill but instead 'Jerky, swerving, water-splashed, it has a quality of panic and urgency'; it is instinctive, unexplained: 'Why does it end that way?' (60). No answer is offered, but this repeated questioning about endings in the story is given shape by the characters' circumstances. As suits a short story, and as many of London's pieces in her collection also suggest, the characters—if they can be nominated such as they are hardly representative of 'human personalities' but instead are as evocatively ephemeral as the fleeting images that comprise cinema they make—are in a state of suspension. They are awaiting the arrival of Steiner, the filmmaker and scriptwriter's lover, who is the measure against which Jacob gauges his present frustrations: '"This is not Steiner's way", he said' (58). Together with an actor, Bernadette, who is engaged to play the role of Nina in Steiner's anticipated filming of *The Seagull*, the three are isolated because of weather events, presented in cinematically epic proportions: 'It was spring, the ice had melted into the rivers, all the bridges were swept away. The telephone lines were down, the ground was too marshy for landings. Steiner was coming in the summer. Summer did not come. For weeks we waited, while it rained' (42). Yet they are also caught, in effect, in an image from Steiner's childhood memory—'He had a memory of a childhood holiday in an old hotel beside a lake' (43)—and they also form an echo of the artists who gather at a country estate in *The Seagull*: just as Treplev writes and has performed unsuccessfully a play within Chekhov's play, the screenwriter sees her project as 'a film within a film' (43). One of the effects of this nesting of narratives, this layering of artifice upon non-reality, is a pulling towards some unknown truth.

London has commented on this aspect of *Letter to Constantine*, telling Jones: 'I aspire to write a myth, to stumble onto something that is so true.'[26] And the ending of 'The Woman Who Only Answered Yes or No' suggests this reach for fidelity, which circles back to the story's opening premise. The narrative opens with the idea that a scriptwriter is being approached for the first time by an implied interviewer, who is addressed in the second person—you—by the first-person narrator: 'Do you know, this is the first time in a long career that I've ever been interviewed. My career? Scriptwriter—other people's scripts' (42). The interview loosens a silence that has settled around a woman's creative endeavours. And it ends with the questioning words of another woman, Berthe, who has, as the title suggests, said little for much of the script-writer's account but who has been the consensual focus of her camera:

> The woman seemed out of breath as she reached me. She put her hand on my arm. '*My film*', she said. Her voice was hoarse, her lips cracked from the sun. She peered into my face. '*When will you finish it? Will you show it in your city? Can I come? Will Steiner see it? Will everybody know then who I am?*' (60–1)

Just as the scriptwriter wonders at the possibility of getting to the truth of her motivations for filming *The Woman* by narrating it to another, Berthe holds out the prospect that cinema will forge connections, and reveal and recognise her true self.

As a volume, *Letters to Constantine* loops around this idea from its titular story: that the art of imagination might afford affirmation and verity. 'The Angry Girl', the collection's penultimate story, also features a female film-maker, Agnes, who, like the medium in which she works, flickers in and out of the narrative, striving to grasp something obscure but sincere by means of her art. As one character observes of Agnes's film: 'something seems to grow in it … it stays' (112). This story is built around the fragmented memories of the first-person narrator—Agnes's former and aging father-in-law—and it turns on the story's initial image: his unexpected glimpse of Agnes in an unfamiliar city street. This sight prompts in the narrator a longing to again see Agnes, whose disappearance from the family and her marriage is hinted at by a collage of recollections that give rise to an uneasy awareness of what the narrator himself does not readily admit, namely an ominous paternalism. London affords this unnamed narrator an emerging share of Agnes' aesthetic vision, thus saving him from the role of a simple despotic male figure. He admits that at the time, when his son and Agnes lived with him and his wife, he could not understand Agnes's cinema: 'all those shots of the same subject from different angles, like a home movie! It seems disjointed, it did not tell a story. Just the things a man—Tony—does in the morning. So what?' (112) London immediately answers this question by means of juxtaposition, narratively enacting the logic of 'shots of the same subject from different angles' so that what her narrator initially determines to be incoherent gives way to lucidity. The narrator's scepticism shifts to understanding as his seeing, both metaphorical and literal, aligns fleetingly with Agnes' cinematic looking:

> It's true that sometimes now in the morning, I see the lines and shapes and shadows in the courtyard, that she filmed Tony watching from the studio. A whole architecture seems to be streaming upwards. For a moment it's as if I see what Tony saw.
>
> Or how Agnes saw him.
>
> …
>
> There is a sense of a secret held within each scene, which she lets stay secret. When I see Tony now I see him in the film. Perhaps that's why I didn't like it. She knew more about him than I did. (112)

As this admission suggests, this story, and London's volume more broadly, takes seriously the possibility that with its capacity to represent 'different angles', creative work, both written and visual, might reveal or fashion an otherwise unacknowledged truthfulness.

Importantly, London's stories are not unaware of the contrivances, and contrariness, that might be involved in such projects. In 'The Woman Who Only Answered Yes or No', Steiner, the filmmaker, authoritatively orders the dismantling of a bar he deems 'inauthentic' to his vision of the set of 'The Seagull', despite it being a community meeting place and a source of income for its proprietor. Small, but meaningful, instances such as this point to how London's stories, for all their dreaminess, are still attuned both to material circumstances and to how the visions of some might well bring damage to others.

In contrast, stories such as 'Angels' and 'Pinch Me, Pinch Me' are altogether inconclusive and are attuned to tone. The sound of a hammer in the first page of 'Pinch Me, Pinch Me' sets that narrative's foreboding register, which finds expression in a woman momentarily kidnapped and uncomprehending of the political currents that have brought her to that situation. 'Angels' ends on a similarly uncertain note. The middle-aged first-person male narrator finds himself with his wife and her friend stuck in a snowed-in car on a road to Scotland. The man is ill, he is pictured gasping for breath, and the narrative approximates the fever-dreams of his sickness. It moves from the present to a vision of a new species of bird, half-admitted failures as a father and husband, and a childhood memory, making the quiet querying that ends the story—'"Isn't this what you've always wanted?" someone whispered. "To die in a woman's arms"' (41)—both knowingly melodramatic and menacing.

Yet, there is an overriding hopefulness in *Letter to Constantine* that the imagination will give meaning and acknowledgment to that which escapes factuality, and this optimism finds clear expression in the collection's two creative biographies: 'The Second Stage' and 'Maisie Goes to India'. Of the eight stories in *Letters to Constantine*, these two narratives take identifiably but very unalike 'real people' as their subjects—the twentieth-century avant-garde Jewish artist, Marc Chagall, and London's mother respectively—and imagine what might have been.

Together in *Letter to Constantine*, the two stories underscore the democratic impulse that runs through the collection. Chagall is a now well-known proto-Surrealist painter; Maisie is a young woman, only momentarily the centre of attention of family members gathered on a quay because she is about to venture to colonial India. Chagall wrote an autobiography in which he gave an account of the first years of his life growing up in the impoverished shtetl of Witebsk in White Russia and his experiences of political and artistic revolution. (Chagall's narrative is released from the gravitational forces of literary convention, much like the fluid, levitating figures in his paintings, so its appeal for London's dream-informed collection is understandable).[27] By contrast, London relates that for Maisie, 'there are no stories about this journey. Like Maisie's childhood in Broome there is only a great silence out of which she makes up stories. This is because, when Maisie was five, her mother died' (125). Yet, these two different lives are valued equally by London, and she approaches the writing of them with a careful respect, alert to how imaginative biography might simplify or impose order on, or indeed misrepresent, a life, but also committed to the idea that such writing can be an honouring act.

The short story is especially disposed to such awareness and dedication because of its parameters. The form makes impossible any presumption to tell of an entire life, and London's focus in each story is on an imagined moment from which her narrative then extends to evoke her subjects' pasts as well as the present time of writing. In 'Maisie Goes to India', London's authorial presence is written into the story by means of interwoven italicised sections that suggest a conversation (or an imagined conversation) she (or the narrator) is having with her mother, and which also serve as a gentle reminder of the limits of what can be known and represented:

> Whenever she sees birds, for some reason she thinks of her mother.
>
> *What did she die of?*
>
> *Blood-poisoning.*

> *How did it happen?*
> *I don't know.*
> *You must know, she was your mother.*
> *You don't know everything about your mother.* (125)[28]

And in 'The Second Stage'—a title slyly acknowledging Chagall's work in theatre as well as the 'first stage' of life he wrote of in *My Life*—London's narrator serves as both painter-author and art historian, establishing and interpreting the invented image of Chagall's unrecorded life:

> You could say what follows takes the form of a painting. A small canvas, a small moment: in a biography it would not earn even more than one line … It's a painting of the back view of a house, of its courtyard and the streetlamp beside it and beyond, a horizon of a thousand mansard roofs … There are no TV aerials; this is Paris, 1923. And there are no lovers loitering beneath the streetlamp. They are in the house, asleep … You can see inside the windows of the house, just make out the figures sleeping in their beds … The woman is asleep … The man beside her is awake … And because he is the only one awake in this sleeping house, it's as if he is the point of consciousness in the painting. As if the whole house, floor by floor, exists through his eyes. (90–1)

The story proceeds as an imagined interregnum in a life. Its small details of impoverishment, hospitality, longing, exile, friendship, and artistic visitations—'At the time the angel's visit through the ceiling seemed hardly surprising, seemed to have its own logic' (102)—are the brushstrokes giving rise to a vision of affirmation that the stories of *Letters to Constantine* collectively realise.

Gilgamesh

As Edith Clark nurses her sleeping child on board the Orient Express, glimpsing light from a stationmaster's lantern as the train travels through the night, she wonders 'What was her story in the great swirling darkness of the world?'[1] That story is *Gilgamesh* (2001), which tells of Edith's search for the father of her child. The book's publication announced the shift of London's creative focus from the short story form to the novel; she would later reflect 'I feel I didn't give up short stories, they deserted me'.[2] As an indication of the esteem in which London's debut novel came to be held, *Gilgamesh* went on to win the 2002 *The Age* Book of the Year for Fiction prize; was shortlisted for the Miles Franklin Literary Award; and was longlisted internationally for both the Orange Prize and the International IMPAC Dublin Literary Award. Initially, however, and as London told the audience at the 2004 Adelaide Writers' Week, one of the earliest responses to the novel was at best lukewarm: 'The first question I was asked two years ago by a radio journalist was if I thought my novel *Gilgamesh*, set roughly between 1918 and 1954, was relevant. My instant and instinctive answer was, "Yes, or I wouldn't have written it"'.[3] 'Relevance' is hardly a neutral term, and what prompted the journalist to pose such a question can only be surmised. But it smuggles in the idea that Australian literature should have practical applications; that it ideally carries out its primary duty to record its own moment or keep within its national borders. *Gilgamesh* eschews such edicts and instead pursues abiding questions about our responsibilities to others.

To do this, the novel takes place around the two world wars of the twentieth century. Edith ventures from her family's Group Settlement farming district in the fictional Nunderup in Western Australia—the place her child was conceived, and which once stood as a postwar promise for returning shell-shocked soldiers—to Armenia, 'the motherland' of her lover, Aram Sinanien (43). Aram was orphaned following the genocidal murder of his family in Turkey in 1915 and Edith believes he has returned there to fight for an independent Armenia. Edith pauses briefly in London on her way to Yerevan, the capital of Armenia, finds momentary refuge in Syria, and finally returns to Nunderup.

The international passage Edith undertakes is not only physical and psychological, familiar-enough ideas for the trope of travel. It is also literary. Stephanie Trigg's thinking about the novel as 'a part of a long and venerable tradition in Australian fiction: a tradition of quest narratives organised around topographic and cultural difference',[4] suggests one lineage, even as the novel questions the authority nations and their narratives command, with the novel registering the senseless carnage inflicted in their names. More immediate for the novel is the Mesopotamian poem *The Epic of Gilgamesh*, a copy of which is read and cherished by London's central characters, in which the hero's quest is ultimately cast as vanity: Gilgamesh, 'a mix of gods' flesh and human', muses near the end of the epic and at the edge of his known world, 'I have filled my sinews with sorrow / and what have I achieved by my toil?'[5] Edith's reflections during the train journey raise similar questions, and call attention to the importance of storytelling within the novel to work towards provisional answers to them.

It is significant, then, that the novel is written in free indirect style, with the narrative largely moving in and around, and merging with, Edith's point of view. One effect of this feature is that the searching question Edith poses on the train regarding her story is both hers and the novel's. Another effect is that the narrative points of view that coalesce around singular characters—Edith's perspective is certainly not the only one represented—are interlaced with something other than themselves. In the face of individual loss and collective atrocity, the plot and patterning of *Gilgamesh*, as Edith intuits and London offers, hold out hope, however momentary, of creating meaning and significant connection, counterposing Edith's sense of her own separateness to the trust that develops and is tested as she comes to rely on the hospitality and resourcefulness of others during her journey.

That Edith's passing eye on board the train is drawn to the stationmaster's lamp is therefore consequential. Earlier in the novel, at home in Nunderup, Edith is herself cast as a sentinel, 'the last to sleep, the first to wake, the watchman of the house' (38). She is also portentous, having unexplained visions of 'her own profile at a train window looking out at some darkening unknown landscape. Someone was with her. Who?' (44). It is perhaps not accidental, then, that the novel itself arose for London from other, different shadows: illness and sleep. When asked in an interview by the author Charlotte Wood how she arrived at the writing of *Gilgamesh*, London related that the experience of breast cancer unexpectedly gave rise to the ideas that would inform her thinking about an unanticipated novel. The diagnosis rearranged London's literary ambitions; she was not consciously working on a new writing project and yet from that experience, *Gilgamesh* part-emerged:

> I just had a lumpectomy, and radiotherapy. Nothing terrible, but it knocked me out. I was completely shocked. I never thought it would happen to me, you know. And in a way *Gilgamesh* came out of that experience, that extremity. It became an enormous journey for me, that time. A determination to pull myself out of this, to survive … Gilgamesh was a cancer novel too, really. A journey of reparation. I guess all our books are symbols of psychic states that we've passed through in some way.[6]

London uses the word 'journey' more than once in this interview to suggest both a will bound to bodily infirmity and the existential edge from which *Gilgamesh* surfaced. And London's novel both literalises the metaphor towards which London reaches to give shape to her experience of illness and seeks for its characters the restitution of which its author speaks. While not wanting to ground the novel too much in London's autobiographical account, Edith's gaze beyond the immediate materiality of her world, directed from the flickering lights and towards the unknowable, resonates in suggestive ways with what London has offered up as another origin of the novel. In the same interview, London tells Wood that dream knowledge gave the novel its starting outline: '*Gilgamesh* came from a dream, which always tells you something about where you are. It's about being lost and making a journey to find what you have lost, and writing it was in itself a sort of journey to affirm myself after the blow to one's being that is having cancer'.[7] When asked to recall the dream, London related:

> Oh gosh, I'm beginning to forget the initial dream, how terrible. It was something about being on a journey—oh, I went to a country, that's right. I went to a strange country surrounded by mountains. It was dark, like a time of war, and I was carrying or leading a small child. There was something I was looking for. And the dream ended with the word 'Gilgamesh'.
>
> I didn't even know what Gilgamesh was, or where it came from. I'd heard of it, vaguely, as a sort of myth. So then I started to research the myth, and then I began to ask, who was that woman with the child, and where did she come from, and what is her place in this myth? What was this country surrounded by mountains, foreign, but not eastern, nor European? I described this country to an erudite Englishman of my acquaintance, and he said: 'It's Armenia.'
>
> ...
>
> It stayed with me. Generally if I dream I've forgotten it by the morning—but this was one of those dreams that stayed with me, it was significant in some way and I wanted to find out what its significance was. Where did I get Gilgamesh from? Had I read about it? It was mysterious. I think that probably only happens once in your life.[8]

It seems apt that London should dream of myth. After all, both myth and dream are arguably tethered to reality but are also not immediately part of that reality. They each can suggest other times while often tasked with providing accounts of the self—as with psychoanalytical approaches to dreams, for instance—or the origin of the world, as the case with myth. Myth and dream have long provided material for writers as both subject matter and aesthetic schema. And in *Gilgamesh*, it is an openness to the mystery that London's dream-myth evoked which underscores the reality London creates for her characters, and in particular for Edith as the novel's protagonist. Very soon after Edith queries her story-to-come at the window of the Orient Express, a textile merchant named Hagop Essayan alights the train—'a black-toothed angel. It was if he had been sent' (119)—and offers her safe passage to Yerevan and unexpected hospitality with an aging poet, Tati, and his polyglot, musical wife, Nevart. Hagop's appearance as a *deus ex machina*—and he is not the only character that takes on this role in the book, as will be discussed—draws out the novel's studied interplay between myth and reality, and an ethics of interdependence.

London confirms for Wood that as part of her approach to writing, she gives specific attention to its mechanics and places special importance on her characters and the authenticity of their worlds:

> It's got to be real, doesn't it? Or you won't accept the allegory. I think the key is the characters. I think characters are everything in writing, actually. It's got to be the characters, and they've got to be as real, as present, as of their time as you can make them. Because you have to feel for them to get involved in the narrative.[9]

The realness of *Gilgamesh*, crafted over years of drafts, discussions and doubt,[10] is that which Edith attributes to

Hagop, namely 'a density behind … lightness' (122), and is also present in the book's physical and temporal setting. *Gilgamesh* is a historical novel insofar as it takes place between the end of the First World War and the mid-1950s, with Edith setting out on her journey to find her child's father in 1939. And it occurs in recognisable locations—rural south-western Australia, London, Armenia, the Middle-East—even as these settings are unfamiliar in significant ways to the time of the novel's writing. As London acknowledged in a talk on *Gilgamesh* as part of the Adelaide Writers' Week in 2004:

> Much of the Australian part of the story was formulated in the area in which it actually takes place, the Margaret River area in the South West, now famous for its wines, vineyards, restaurants and surf and a major tourist destination … There couldn't be a greater contrast between this playground of the rich as the South West has become, and what it was: an impoverished dairying area carved of the tall timber in the 1920's by a government scheme called Group Settlement, in which a group of 10 or 12 settlers, mainly ex-servicemen, English and Australian, were each given a parcel of land, 12 cows and a bank loan to pay it all off.
>
> …
>
> Edith's farm has been reduced to a home paddock, the rest sold off to a neighbouring hotel, the Sea House, which is based on a real hotel, still extant, in the area, Caves House where from the early 1900s, couples would spend their honeymoon, as my parents did, in the 1930's. And I think that in setting the book in its time-frame, I was exploring my parents' generation, a generation that lives through two world wars and the Depression, and the values of that

time, of thrift, hard work, honesty, church and the lurking parental presence of the British ... These of course were all the values that had formed my generation and against which we rebelled.

I think there's always a certain edginess in writing of the past from the perspective of the present, that undercuts any nostalgia.[11]

That London is acutely aware of the force of the present in the past her novel represents is suggested by her return to this idea in other public talks. In a session for the 2003 Perth Writers' Festival, for example, London raised and commented on the same concern she would discuss a year later in Adelaide:

Even though the novel covers a time from the end of the First World War till after the Second, into the fifties, I became aware that issues such as childrearing, class, white settlement, Aboriginal displacement, the psychological effect of genocide on subsequent generations, implicitly reflect the cultural attitudes of the late-twentieth/early-twenty-first century. However 'old' your story is, it will bear the stamp of your own age.[12]

And yet, the reality of both the present and past of which London writes knowingly in *Gilgamesh* also has room in it for the inexplicable, the coincidental and the condition of hope, the centripetal forces that support Edith's journeying to Armenia and return to Nunderup. Coupled with London's fidelity to the real is her turn to the imagination; a productive coalition that London acknowledges as playing an important part in the writing of *Gilgamesh*. As she told a Canadian audience in 2003:

> Because I thought that I would never get to Armenia [London eventually travelled there with her husband, Geoffrey, as part of her research in October 1997] I'd already written a version of Edith's time there, and in essence, in the narrative and emotional dynamic, that version did not change. I already had an Armenia in my head. *That* Armenia lay like a palimpsest over the actual Armenia: and, as much as I sought out all the actual historic monuments, I was also keeping an eye for the locations of my imagination, apartments, parks, cafes. I was also inhabiting Edith's city. The real Armenia didn't take away from the city, it added to it, added touches and shades, gave me new ideas. In the end the two Armenias merged into the novel.[13]

As much as London is concerned with historical reality, her writing calls for attention to how this reality is imaginatively represented. Subtle narrative patterning, a quiet recurrence of motifs such as the anticipated train journey and the multiple so-called minor characters that step in to assist Edith with her quest, is important for this realistic effect as well as narrative density and complexity. Afforded by the free indirect style of the novel, this design brings a spatial element to the narrative that accords with Edith's travelling. It stitches together fleeting moments that comprise and give shape to the quest Edith undertakes and cast her as the novel's primary focus.

In thinking about Edith as the book's protagonist, it is helpful to acknowledge that from early in the novel, she is figured as an outsider due to poverty and geography, and also by an inherited mix of shame, despair and pride that has its origins in both her English mother's griefs for a lost infant son and a lost home, and her father's sense that he has failed to realise the future vision he had promised Ada when they met in a convalescent war hospital in London: 'Fresh air, honest toil, taking orders from no man … light so clear you seem to swim in it' (6). In Nunderup, Ada and Frank Clark shyly shun their neighbours, 'they were known in the district, didn't go to the dances or the pictures' (8) and, following Frank's early death, Edith's sister Frances carries on the family's self-respecting but also pained separateness, telling her sister that their father 'wouldn't like' the teenage Edith working for Madge Tehoe, the owner of the neighbouring hotel, the Sea House (30). Edith is pragmatic and quietly defiant, however. The family is destitute and Edith is increasingly curious about the world, an inquisitiveness that the unexpected arrival in Nunderup of Aram and Edith's English cousin, Leopold, hints at. Visitors to the Sea House, whom she silently serves, afford Edith another glimpse of life beyond Nunderup, and additionally, and unknowingly, provide the trinkets she unapologetically pockets to painstakingly fund the ocean voyage she plans in secret for her infant son and herself. It is telling that the coins she gathers evoke that which is discarded at sea, both anticipating Edith's voyage and telling something of how she is positioned in her small society:

> She'd never noticed how much money people left lying around before. Not only tips, which, swift and efficient, she hunted down as soon as guests booked out. But pennies, threepences, little mounds of shilling pieces, rolled around in chair backs, drawers, under cushions, in the dust beneath the beds. Small change was the flotsam of the world. Edith made sure at least twice a day that she walked past the

> telephone in the hall, where there was often a few coins. She handed some of them in of course, in case Madge had set a trap. (81)

The novel never leaves its readers in doubt about its sympathies for Edith. As she finally sets sail from Fremantle harbour bound for England, Edith's donning of Madge's brown velour hat, which she impulsively filches at the end of her last shift at Sea House, is quietly humorous and triumphant, and a sign of the value she, and the novel, has in the discarded and the overlooked.

The journey Edith undertakes constitutes part of the novel's story and is marked as exceptional. Edith herself has private qualms about her decision: 'Where did the idea come from, to go to Armenia? Such a preposterous idea, in a place where most of Edith's generation, the children of the settlers, had never even been to Perth … Where those like Ada, who had come here from other countries, were never able to go back. Who had even heard of Armenia?' (74). And these doubts are confirmed by the hotelier Madge whose expression of incredulity at the news Edith has left Nunderup slides into a choral voice, that of the farming community: '"I don't believe you," Madge said. "Where *is* Armenia again?" … Word got around, but nobody really believed that Edith had gone to Armenia. Wherever on earth that was' (85). For Edith, Armenia figures as a non-place onto which her desires are projected; she comes to realise in the streets of Yerevan that Armenia 'belonged, if anywhere back home' (134). But if Edith's decision to leave is cast as improbable, it also involves a sloughing off of a constriction of imagination linked with small country places and characters. (The dream

Leopold has of Nunderup, in which 'everyone looked hardened and narrow-minded, xenophobic, graceless to the point of denial of all beauty' (48) while unfair to the settler residents of Nunderup, nevertheless captures an idea of Australian country towns that the novel purposefully entertains to distinguish its protagonist.) But the journey undertaken by the restless and enquiring Edith is more than a result of her individual determination; it is furnished by ideas of romance that the novel turns to and negotiates.

As a term variously used in the so-called western literary tradition to describe medieval narratives featuring courtly knights and chivalric heroes, and which combined components of morality and magic; a genre of prose fiction that emerged alongside imperialism in the nineteenth century to denote adventurous, exotic tales of journeying; and complicated stories that can be dated from at least the second and third centuries and which have love as the motivating action and affect, romance takes on many forms. And it is arguably the case that each finds overlapping expression in *Gilgamesh* to give shape to a story that comes into view out of the 'whirling darkness' to which Edith looks intently for possibilities.

Gilgamesh has a special interest in the potential, as well as the limitations, that romance narratives hold for Edith. Leopold might echo his aunt's despair that '*There is no romance in this country*' (48), yet London's book has very different ideas. From the novel's outset and from the point of view of their newly arrived cousin, both Edith and her sister are conceived of as 'such serious girls. Mute, stiff, thin, their hair pinned back and plaited like schoolgirls, their faces childishly bare' (24). They are unlikely romantic heroines—rigid rather than agile; sexless rather than desiring. But the novel repeatedly tests the conventions of romance, with *The Epic of Gilgamesh* just one of its part-models and subjects. As London herself glosses this tale in her notes for a talk in Canada:

> The epic of Gilgamesh, which gives the title to my novel, and provides a sort of leit-motif, is the first narrative poem in world literature, and also the first great travel story. Gilgamesh was the young king of Uruk in ancient Mesopotamia, who may or may not have actually existed nearly 3000 years BC. On the death of his friend Enkidu, Gilgamesh sets off on a great journey to find the secret of eternal life. In the prologue [Tablet 1: The Coming of Enkidu][14] we are told: *He saw what was secret, discovered what was hidden/ he brought back a tale of before the Deluge/ He came a far road, was weary, found peace/ all his labours were set on a tablet of stone*. So Gilgamesh was also a writer, giving us a report of all he had learnt. It seems that the journey as a vehicle for learning is as old as storytelling itself. Gilgamesh, from having been such an arrogant, aggressive young kid that the gods conspire to teach him a lesson, returns home older and sadder, to accept his mortal status and responsibilities, and become a just and wise king.[15]

The novel's referencing of *The Epic of Gilgamesh* is explicit and so asks readers to give considered thought to its importance. At first, this epic is associated with Aram and Leopold who 'met in Iraq, where Leopold was working on an archaeological dig, not far from Baghdad, on the Euphrates. Aram was working for the expedition as a driver … In Aram's taxi they drove all across Mesopotamia, visiting other sites, ancient cities, Ur, Larsa, Nineveh, Uruk, buried beneath the sands' (26).

Their introduction is quickly rehearsed in the narrative for the benefit of Leopold's Australian cousins (and the reader), and immediately connects the men with the Gilgamesh epic as it was at the site of Nineveh that clay tablets inscribed with the story were discovered.

This connection is insisted upon throughout the novel, but with telling carefulness. Aram and Leopold 'spoke of Gilgamesh is if they knew him' (41) and 'joked about him, as if he were still alive, as if he were their hero' (54). Gilgamesh and the associated epic haunt the text and portend: Enkidu, Gilgamesh's companion, is killed by the gods and Gilgamesh is left with enveloping grief and a quest for immortality, as Edith part-remembers, recalling the friendships at once, both the real and the mythological: 'One of them dies … Which one? What happened next?' (54)

Yet the repetition of the conjunction 'as if' in the description of Aram and Leopold's imagined fellowship with the mythic character gives pause, suggesting both familiarity with, and some cautious distance from, the figure of Gilgamesh. Further, and beyond the likeness or difference that 'as if' equally affords, the phrase also lets in imagination: the circumstances might not be true, but they are possible. In a corresponding manner, London's novel cannot be said to simply follow or replay the epic it references in its title and throughout its narrative. It certainly leaves aside the epic's exalted register. And it would be limiting to equate characters in *Gilgamesh* with those in the epic. If such a game were to be taken up, it might be said, as a start, that Edith variously plays the parts of Gilgamesh (in her quest and her mourning), Enkidu (in her entry into the netherworld), and Ishtar (the goddess of love). But these identifications would miss how London's novel opens out into narrative inventiveness to position the epic, much as the characters do, as a companion rather than a prescription.

London layers her narrative in such a manner so that what is said about Aram and Leopold, and indeed Gilgamesh the king, is oftentimes filtered through Edith's romantic point of view, as naïve at times as it is clear-eyed at others. In a manner of instruction, Leopold shares with Edith (and consequently the reader), the history and story of Gilgamesh, both the man and the epic: 'The world's oldest known work of poetry. Gilgamesh was the king of Uruk in the land of Sumer. He was supposed to have lived about three thousand years BC … Please, read it if you're interested' (41). Leopold and Aram embody the epic's promise of adventure, its warning about hubris, and its celebration of male friendship:

> They said it was a last-minute decision. They had been travelling together through the Middle East. They met some sailors in a restaurant in Aden, who invited them to take berth on their ship to Australia. They had a little money left, and no immediate obligations, and they said why not. Leopold had always wanted to meet the antipodean branch of his family. (26)

Significantly, the spontaneity and mobility the two men assume, and the notions of time with which they are associated, are not shared by the novel's young women for whom such conditions are simply unavailable. Later in the narrative Edith pointedly reminds her cousin that in *The Epic of Gilgamesh*, 'nothing happens' to the women: 'It's not their story. No woman goes off on quests like that. Women get stuck. They are left behind with the children' (176). Edith is interested in the heroic but unlike her cousin and his friend, she is alert to how narratives might carry gendered conventions and expectations, which London's *Gilgamesh* rescripts.

Like *The Epic of Gilgamesh*, but with a knowing purpose that it attributes to its protagonist, London's *Gilgamesh* imagines Edith's circumstance initially as one of stasis—'she can't leave, she has nowhere else to go' (49)—and qualified by ideas of popular romance. These notions are cultivated by the incuriosity of others and give shape to the young woman's self-perceptions: 'nobody asked about her plans … she knew she longed for shallowthings, plucked eyebrows, high heels, waved hair. Icecream, the boogie-woogie, a pink satin quilted dressing-gown. A big hot cinema smelling of sweat and hair oil and chocolate' (44). What unfolds from this romantic scenario Edith has imagined—this image is resolutely not that of Nunderup with its scarcities—is the fleeting and somewhat chaste idea of marriage that the narrative offers and which, in terms of narrative structure, immediately follows Aram and Edith's sexual union: 'He kissed her on the forehead and took her hand. They set off down the track, silent as if returning from a ceremony' (46). And yet, from this point, this near-beginning, Edith is half-aware that such a vision of romance and its implied futurity is perhaps impossible, too, in the face of historical catastrophe and interminable personal loss. As she will become aware, Hagop's marriage to Nevart, for one, is 'a marriage of convenience' (127), with both characters damaged physically and psychologically by political purges and violent unrest. Later in the novel, this inkling is further suggested by Edith who, in confused transit at Istanbul's Sirkeci train station, briefly sees 'newlyweds holding hands at the dusty kerb, about to disappear forever into the teeming crowd' (120). It is an image that recurs and recedes throughout the novel, and partially comes to rest on a painful understanding Edith arrives at when Leopold gently admits that Aram 'never spoke of the personal. He'd once said that in the orphanage you had to hide what you wanted to keep for yourself … So, no words of undying passion. Nothing to justify her journey' (181). The trauma Aram carries has him isolated and alienated, at least as Leopold tells it: 'Aram was a survivor. What did he know of families, of mothers or sisters? He didn't feel he really belonged in the world' (182). In contrast, and with her very different history, Edith represents a tentative hopefulness.

The novel acknowledges subtly that Edith's past and present are founded on the catastrophe of colonialism, of which she is the part-knowing beneficiary. The 'settling' of the land in Western Australia, which is at the heart of the betrothal promise Frank makes to Ada when in England, is initially imbued in the text with a postwar pioneering spirit that would not be out of place in a late-nineteenth-century colonial romance: 'Frank joined a government scheme to open up the wilds of south-western Australia. Land, parcelled into blocks, was given to a group of twenty or thirty settlers who would initially work together to clear each home block and build each other a house' (7). But Edith is shown to be ashamed of her ignorance when asked by Leopold, in the guise of an ethnographer—he reads Robert Louis Stevenson's *In the South Seas*—'And were there native peoples that the experiment had displaced?" (34) The text's near silence on the massacre of Indigenous families and their displacement from their ancestral lands and waters arguably models Edith's professed unawareness of what she cannot intellectually register but sensorially gleans: 'And didn't she, didn't all of them, sense something in the bush, a presence they didn't understand?

That made them suspect they didn't really know this land at all' (34). Far more than inferred, though, Indigenous women are resolutely, if fleetingly, present in the novel. As London acknowledged in a 2004 talk at the Adelaide Writers' Week:

> … whatever writers wish to write is dictated by the present, by their current state of mind: consciously or unconsciously writers select settings that enable them to pursue themes and issues of relevance to their lives in the present … To write of the bush now, it's impossible to leave out the Aboriginal ownership of the land, their presence or the reason for their lack of presence, as was done in so many of the narratives written at the time. And impossible also not to mention and explore a little the unease in the relationship that white Australians have with the bush: a passionate love, but a sense of being an outsider: a distrust deep down of their right to belong there.[16]

Edith, heavily pregnant, sees an Indigenous woman with a child and wonders at the possibility of a shared experience in a way that might be read as both an attempt at understanding and a fantasy of solidarity that sidesteps the women's real historical and cultural differences. Even at this moment of imagined connection, the novel recognises how colonial presumptions prevail, and are perhaps even written into aspects of the romance narratives on which the novel rests. While the lives and losses of the Indigenous women and their families are inferred, Frances has no second thoughts about 'plans for crops and a piggery … to fulfil her father's dream' (226), for example, and the woman does not appear again.

Within the logic of the text's looping temporality, Frances seems fated to complete her father's colonial enterprise and Jim is resolved to see Leopold and to repeat, with a difference, his mother's questing journey to forestall loss. As with *The Epic of Gilgamesh*, loss permeates the novel and it is what Edith modestly and implicitly proposes to vanquish by means of her love for her son. This claim might seem grandiose or misguided given the novel's attention to histories of violence that have contributed significantly to such finalities and unending bereavements. But, for all her questing to recover Aram, it is her determination to keep her son close, to not lose him, that offers some modest shape of a future rising up from the grief that resolutely marks the novel (and which Gilgamesh, in the epic, cannot reconcile himself to as he mourns Enkidu.) Edith's mother, Ada, is orphaned as a child; on her move to Australia with Frank following the war she loses her home; once in Nunderup her infant son dies, leaving her inconsolable and misunderstood by her gentle husband, who also dies too soon. Ada's sister-in-law and Leopold's mother, Irina, loses a husband and brother to war. Edith's companion in Yerevan, Tati, 'had survived the Turkish Massacres, the Great War, the Communist purges of the thirties. She had lost everyone' (138), and the director of the orphanage on Aleppo's outskirts, where Leopold, Jim and Edith take shelter, and where Aram lived as a child, 'was the only survivor of her family. All the rest had died in the death marches of 1915' (185). Aram, too, has lost his family as well as any childhood memory he might have once had of his mother. He cannot recall his past but for what he has been told of it by others:

> When he was three years old Turkish gendarmes had come, taken his father to the city square and hanged him. He and his mother were marched in a convoy of women and

> children across the desert to Syria. By the time they reached the Euphrates, his mother, like most of the convoy, was dead ... I don't remember this, he said. I don't remember my mother. I don't remember any of it. (45)

Edith is also confronted by the possibility of loss (albeit in very different circumstances) from the moment of Jim's birth: she spirits him away from the lying-in hospital before he can be adopted; much later, she secures his release from a facility beyond Nunderup to which Frances commits him as an adolescent in his mother's absence. Her love for him is offered up as the novel's counterpoint to loss. At a moment of quiet reckoning, with the world at war and Edith and Jim reunited in Syria not with Aram but Leopold, Edith's admission that she set out into the world 'for Jim's sake. Well, all right, I did it for love' (176) is suggestively ambiguous. One implication of this confession is that the love she speaks of here is of her feeling for her son rather than, or at least co-existent with, the image of romantic love for Aram in which she had cast her quest.

For a significant part of the story, Edith holds onto the notion that the romance narrative she imaginatively bears will be realised. She rehearses her finding of Aram in the ready-made terms of romance: 'Again and again she enacted it, finding him, standing before him, confronting him with Jim. And then of course he would hold his arms out to them, and they would have a home at last' (74). It is a stock image, and 'of course' strikes a telling note here. This phrase suggests some wariness about a fantasised reconciliation between Edith and Aram, with the effect being that the romance trope of happily ever after is held up as knowingly predictable, and gently mocked. Yet, if London admits this prosaism amid her character's thoughts, she continues to have Edith persist with this romantic ideal in the face of what the novel presents as reality's 'hard edge' (5). Aunt Irina is alert to the impending war and angrily voices her disbelief at the younger woman's professed motivations to travel to Armenia from London, where she, a displaced White Russian, now lives:

> 'You are going for love', Irina said. '*Love!* People die, not for love, but for hate where you are going. Do you know how many Jews are trying to get into England at the moment? You are leaving a sanctuary to go into the heart of a maelstrom. Love is a luxury. To die for love is a romantic luxury in the modern world' ... 'You know, Edith,' said Irina softly, deadly, 'no good ever came from chasing a man.' (106)

The world at war intrudes on the novel's romances yet Edith's response gathers into itself a sense of immortality that Gilgamesh in the epic seeks (and ultimately fails to find, thanks to a serpent that eats the plant which had promised him the secret to ever-lasting life). Edith tells her aunt, 'I'm not going to die ... and neither is Jim' (106). The merchant Hagop strengthens this conviction, telling Edith later in the narrative as he confirms for her Aram's death and the immediate need for her evacuation of Yerevan, 'You and Jim must live' (166). This repetition, and insistence, has the effect of a talisman.

The novel's concern with Edith's survival is therefore also a complex meditation on time and existence that complicates the linear narrative trajectory nominally ascribed to the amorous form of romance by Aunt Irina's word 'chase', to tell the stories Edith's wonders at while facing 'the great swirling darkness of the world'. While the narrative does not occupy Aram's point of view, the impression left is that his thoughts traverse the unknowable past and future; the sensual present in which he lives in the house with Edith, her sister and mother is of little consequence. In the rare times when the narrative point of view moves away from Edith and toward Leopold, who has his own mixed, half-surfaced feelings towards his cousin, Aram is pictured differently and in a way that punctures Edith's idea of the two as Gilgamesh and Enkidu, the firmest of friends:

> He only knew him as a traveller. Who took what he needed but needed little. Water, a bedroll, tobacco. The occasional woman … He travelled light, like a warrior. He didn't take what he couldn't carry (48).

Edith gleans that the weeks Aram 'spent with her were not important to him … All this time, he'd been really thinking of something else' (46): his mother dead, his failure to remember, his desire to defend Armenia. Instead, their intimacy is imbricated in the historical time which the men's guide of *The Epic of Gilgamesh* foretells and which also has a part in motoring the epistemological compulsion of narrative that Edith senses as she remembers indistinctly the epic's plot and tries to remember which man dies. It is Aram, whose point of view the narrative does not enter, who is always already absent; his eventual death is rumoured but assumed to be true. In contrast, Leopold is given a form of resurrection. Having facilitated safe passage for Edith and Jim out of Yerevan following their search for Aram, Edith believes her cousin dead, killed by a bomb she hears explode at some distance from their sanctuary. Yet, he writes to her years later, setting in motion the next generation's quest with Jim, now grown, closing the novel by heading to

Baghdad to visit his relative, suggesting a coiling of experience and time. This jumble of timelines, captured by Edith's efforts to call to mind a future already told and her desire to know what happens next, echoes the complex temporality with which Aram and Leopold are similarly associated in the novel.

The time of these two men is also yoked expressly with the past and the end of time: 'They buried themselves in the ancient world. Because, of course, the whole modern world was about to erupt. That, they said, was what was waiting for them at the end of their travels' (26). For Leopold and Aram, their time in Nunderup is a temporal pause before an anticipated abyss; for Edith, it is a beginning, a new time, as she starts to imagine what might be possible beyond Nunderup 'because her old life was coming to an end' (91). And the narrative form itself is faithful to this complex conception, and intersection, of time and being. At one moment, Leopold is pictured saying his farewells to Edith right before he boards a bus; the next, the two are discussing *The Epic of Gilgamesh* in the days before the men's departure. And one of the impressions left in the novel by this montage effect and London's free indirect style—an invitation to see Edith through her own eyes but also to have access to more than what the character can know at the time—is that while Edith's viewpoint is the focus, a future time is also present; London's writing feels involved in, and sympathetic to, the story it is telling. The narrative times of London's *Gilgamesh* contract and expand to tell Edith's story which both defies and depends upon the intertwined plots and tropes of the heroic romance and the love romance.

Edith's determination to journey to Armenia to find Aram is a resolve that unites these two romantic possibilities, but it is also dismantled in such a way that both narratives are rescripted to admit ruminations on Edith's vulnerability and the importance of openness to otherness. The ocean journey Edith sets out on is imperceptibly prompted by the intimate knowledge of her pregnancy, with the novel turning to simile to glimpse that connection. Edith's experience of quickening is beautifully told of as 'like a sail across the sea' (53). For herself and Jim, her baby, Edith books passage on a cargo ship bound for England, but only after she purposefully rejects both the tacit expectation that, as an unwed young woman, she will relinquish her child and the scripts of small-town life that would otherwise determine her destiny.

The first part of her journey foreshadows the hospitality, and threats to it, that she will encounter as she makes her way to Armenia. On board, she is offered a space of her own, but this gesture is undercut by a sailor who trespasses one night into her cabin and stands before not Edith but Jim, 'His hand was at his crotch, moving rhythmically up and down' (95–6). Edith's passage with Jim on the Orient Express is then marked by an encounter with a monied Armenian man who summons Edith to his compartment to share 'a glass of sherry [and] a little company' (113) after having observed her from afar. But in this space of heightened sexual threat, she meets Hagop, who furnishes her journey and residency in Yerevan yet who also, it is later suggested by Leopold, might be on a retainer from the same man from whose lechery she believes Hagop has assisted her to evade.

London's novel does not therefore simply replay these narratives and their events in a way that figures Edith as a straightforward romantic heroine. Edith does eventually come to a tentative understanding and affection with a man, Lawrence Ford, a communist and a farmer. Attending the local cinema with Lawrence to see *From Here to Eternity* late in the novel, Edith wonders inwardly about her earlier leaning on romance to make sense of her world and determines 'That was all in the past. In the Busselton Open-Air Cinema, 1954, she existed on a very different plane'. Lawrence concurs in his own way: 'Hysterical Yankee patriotism' is his unimpressed assessment of the film (237). And she does return to Nunderup, the classic quest journey seemingly realised, with Edith inevitably, insofar as the narrative framework would have it, arriving both 'home' and at the knowledge that 'for her the great adventure was now to stay' (255). For Jim, however, whose third-person point of view the last part of the novel comes to privilege, the experience of return is more complicated: 'he didn't know what home meant. To him it was just another border, the queues on the wharf, the men in uniforms, the corrugated iron shed … Theirs was just one story among hundreds of sagas reaching an end here' (191). This restlessness marks his youth and propels his departure, which is the novel's conclusion.

So, in those capacities, Edith does fulfil the roles made for her by the overlapping quest and love romance narratives, and for a reader wanting a heroine who strides out into the world and stays there, shunning men and the trappings of domesticity, Edith deeply disappoints. Yet, what the novel intriguingly, and tellingly, removes for Edith to come to such 'conclusions' are those obstacles that ordinarily both delay and put to the test the questing hero and the desiring lover alike, and motor the plot of romance narratives.

Edith certainly has agency; she steals the spare change at Sea House and has no hesitation in raiding her Aunt Irina's cupboards to make nappies from the sheets she determines her host 'would not miss' (107). And she suffers hardships in her travels that Hagop's wife Nevart in Yerevan perhaps puts in context but also makes a matter of competitiveness between the two women: 'Did you ever eat rats or dogs like the peasants did here during the collectivisation? The stuffing from an armchair? Grass soup?' (145). At the same time, Edith is held safe by a narrative motif of unexplained and fortuitous encounters that take the place of the impediments to be overcome which would usually distinguish romances.

It is a risky narrative device for London to deploy. After all, *deus ex machina* is a contentious staple of select Greek drama. Euripides, the tragedian, most notably turned to divine intervention to untangle and settle his play's plots. So, by those terms, its place in a romance narrative such as *Gilgamesh* is already suspect.[17] Also, the world of *Gilgamesh* is one in which contact with the gods is tenuous at best. The elderly Tati's declaration that 'God had sent Edith to her' (145) is met by Nevart's eye-rolling. Miss Anoosh, the orphanage director, is a woman of faith in whose room, adorned with an Armenian Orthodox wooden cross, Edith finds momentary comfort. But Frances's uttering of the belief that 'there is but one God' (42), in response to a discussion about the gods in *The Epic of Gilgamesh*, is met with surprise by Edith who 'had never heard her mention God before' (42); much later in the novel, Frances's piety is taken advantage of by fraudsters who peddle faith in the hope of gaining access to property rights. In a different register, but one that nevertheless conjures the secularisation of the divine, Hagop's world, a smoky bar of hinted-at radical politics and espionage, is to Edith 'the *underworld*' (where Enkidu is forever held in *The Epic of Gilgamesh*) but to Hagop 'heaven' (156). If *Gilgamesh* has gods at all, they are certainly not interventionist: Nevart falls out of a hotel window to her death without reason or explanation, and in wartime '[y]oung men in slouch hats and khaki' are 'slaughtered and maimed' (139).

Furthermore, the *deus ex machina* generally suffers from an enduring aesthetic animosity directed against it. Such distrust and distaste are thanks largely to Aristotle, who argued that the denouement, that which follows a plot's climax and works towards resolution, must emerge from the action. Within this framework, which has come to shape literature and expectations of it for over a millennia, appearing unexpectedly out of nowhere the *deus ex machina* and its plot resolutions are regarded as artificial and artless. Yet, in the skilful hands of London and in the romance narratives of *Gilgamesh*, such interventions are not directed at plot solutions but are rather rehearsed in the service of the novel's ethical thinking.

The substitution, as it were, of obstacles with *deus ex machina* in the romance plots of *Gilgamesh* means that the compulsion to 'overcome', which so often drives such narratives and which *The Epic of Gilgamesh* sees as futile, is displaced by a valuing of trust; a necessary openness to others; and the capacity of narrative to give shape to the chaos of experience. In addition to the unbidden and unexpected appearances of Hagop and Leopold, who steer Edith through, and away from, dangers, Edith and Jim find their way back to Australia from Syria serendipitously; they 'joined an Australian transport bound for Palestine. It happened by chance' (187); Edith and Jim's initial encounter with the Caucasus is described in a similar way: 'By some fluke or magic, she, Edith Clark, had slipped across the line, left the safety of the pink territory and crossed over into the vast unknown green' (125). Edith herself seems not to recognise this recurrent narrative design that affords chance significance. In Yerevan, in the courtyard of the small apartment she comes to share with Tati and Nevart, Edith accounts for her capacity to endure in terms of self-reliance: 'Only her childhood solitude had allowed her to survive' (159). In a similar vein, she later counsels Jim: 'Never let yourself fall into a stranger's hands' (218). And yet the novel suggests otherwise. At the same time it depicts Edith as understanding her search for Aram as a romantic quest, which calls on her resources as a self-sufficient individual, the novel offers this representation to explore ideas of intersubjectivity. As part of this consideration, *Gilgamesh* comes to insist that others have a part to play in Edith's survival, as does she to them.

London's story is full of strangers and visitors. The visitors to the Sea House in Nunderup are inadvertently central to Edith's journey, and the rest of the novel features meaningful encounters with others. Structurally, *Gilgamesh* is composed of five parts, and the first line of the second of these, titled 'Visitors', announces 'Strangers ride into town' (19). The novel ends on a similar note: Edith imagines Jim as a stranger to Leopold, 'he would raise his head as the stranger comes into the café' before 'the gleam of recognition kindling in his eyes' (255–6). That initial sentence of the novel's second section introduces Aram and Leopold into the novel; highlights the interest of *Gilgamesh* in travel and outsiders; and tells of the hospitality of others that the figure of the stranger evokes and relies on in this story. The point of view that first records the two young men is omniscient and familiar, reporting that 'Here they come, in a cloud of dust, bumping over the gravel on the road to Nunderup' (19). Very soon it becomes apparent that the dust cloud is not caused by heavy footsteps, as might first be inferred, but rather by the tyres of 'an old Ford utility' (19) whose driver then focalises the narrative and ask the question, on behalf of London's readers:

> Where had they come from? The cab was filled with the foreign smell of them. Bickford knew it, he had served in Egypt in the AIF ... Close up they were young, mid-twenties. Officer age and class. One was wiry, dark as a Gyppo, the other fat, spoke like a Pom. What had brought them here? They weren't the type to work in the timber mills. Out of the corner of his eye Bickford watched the fat one wipe the sweat from his hands with his neckscarf. Soft hands like that on a man turned his stomach. (19)

Mr. Bickford, a farmer, casts the two men as resolutely different from himself: they are foreign and effeminate. And to underscore the point, as well as the chapter's initial nomination of them as 'strangers', he reflects that, 'He wouldn't have said no to a beer if they'd offered to shout him one, but they were foreigners and didn't know the way to do things around here' (21). For all his unthinking recourse to crude stereotype, however, Bickford enacts a hospitality that is a concern of the novel throughout. Bickford's reflections on the strangers he transports in his truck emerge in response to what *Gilgamesh* seems to suggest is Leopold's misrecognition of the meaning of Bickford's assistance. Leopold, unidentified at this point in the narrative, presents Bickford with 'five shillings for the ride, but Bickford shook his head' (21). With the offer of money, Leopold proposes a transactional encounter; Bickford's refusal points to a hospitality that is of a different order of value, and it is one that the novel comes to privilege. The strangers might provoke a shudder of visceral revulsion in Bickford, but he nevertheless extends to them momentary support without expectation of anything (except perhaps a beer) in return. This form of hospitality turns on complex relations between characters who slip between positions of visitor and host during the narrative, which does not so much resolve such interactions or pin down their meanings as instate, and make important, their primacy in the novel's romances.

It is surely salient that the poet, Tati, articulates this idea in a way that echoes, but rescripts, her visitor's earlier claims about her apparent existential endurance:

> 'You have kept me alive, Edith,' Tati said. 'You and Jim. *Hokvov yev marmenov*. Body and soul.'
>
> Edith and Jim, buttoned up, their scarves across their faces, paused at the door.
>
> 'But alive for what?' Tati went on, as if to herself. 'For death? For one more poem? *The* poem, at last?' She chuckled, wheezing and waved her hand. Goodbye. *Hadjo!* Good luck.' (165)

Tati extends hospitality to Edith and her son who have arrived at her apartment in Yerevan as strangers. Edith reciprocates, offering Tati not only intimate physical care but also gentleness: 'By mid-morning she would have Tati sitting in her chair … washed and fed, her white hair brushed, her hands on her lap, her high cheekbones dusted with powder. This was Edith's task … To give Tati form, bring her back into the world for one more day' (137). And Tati extends more than physical shelter to her guests. She also forwards for the novel a way of thinking about the self and relationships with others that rests on a recognition of interdependency but also leaves unanswered the questions this arrangement generates. The proposition that there might be an answer, '*the* poem', the one that explains it all or realises an aesthetic ideal, is laughed at. But at the same time, Tati's turn to art as that which might be something meaningful and might also ward off death, for a while, is captured in her wish for Edith and Jim. Luck, after all, is what London's *Gilgamesh* provides these two characters with and is another name for the hospitality and succour that others repeatedly offer Edith and Jim, affirming the coda throughout the novel that they will not die.

While strangers in the novel do certainly present to Edith and Jim as threats—the sailor and the Armenian businessman on the Orient Express are two—Tati sees in the figure of the stranger alternative possibilities that take on an urgent force in the time of war the characters are living through. As Hagop tells Edith: 'England and France had declared war on Germany. Ten days ago Russia had signed a non-aggression pact with Germany. "You and I, Edith, are officially at war"' (138). Around them nation states are fighting wars founded on lethal difference and in this circumstance the hospitalities the characters extend to each other, oftentimes with deep ambivalence—Nevart fiercely begrudges Edith's presence but nevertheless comes to rely on her for assistance—and not without prejudice, as Bickford's inner remarks suggest, are a crucial, valued counterpoint to this violence.

The novel petitions its characters to come to a respectful understanding of the limits of extending and accepting hospitality, and to loving others, and these find expression in the mother–son relationship at its heart. Edith might continue to minister care to the elderly on her return to Nunderup, just as she had done for Tati in Yerevan. But, her primary focus, as it has been throughout, is Jim. As she tells Lawrence on their first date, 'I look after my son' (232), a claim that echoes Jim's self-awareness that 'Home was Edith wherever they went. He was filled with a childish longing for her. He couldn't remember spending a night apart from her before' (215). Yet it is Lawrence, who has little time for romance, who tenderly speaks to Edith the novel's counsel: 'Let him be' (244). These words concern Jim as much as Leopold, who Edith has thought dead and mourned, and whose unexpected letter sets out the futures for mother and son. Leopold writes: '*Do you still have the book of Gilgamesh? It's a consolation sometimes to think that thousands of years ago, men knew about all this. The return … If I trust my intuition … I would say that you, Edith, have found your place by now. And Jim? At seventeen, at the start of it all? Perhaps in need of some new horizons*' (253). The return here refers to the reappearance of Leopold, Edith's return to Nunderup and a romantic relationship, and Jim's inheritance of the romance quest. It suggests, too, a repeating and foretelling that is the substance of myth and the patterning of *Gilgamesh* itself.

The Good Parents

The Good Parents (2008) was on London's mind for some time before she started writing it. In mid-November 2001, with *Gilgamesh* published, Joan London began a new notebook with the handwritten entry:

> Once in a winter twilight a schoolgirl was waiting for a bus beside a wet highway when a stranger pulled up and offered her a lift. And without a word, or hardly a moment's hesitation, the girl, Toni Parker, climbed in.
>
> Why did she do it? She was going to have to think about this for the rest of her life.
>
> There are times in her life when she is forced to think about this and she doesn't care much to. She comes up with different answers.
>
> So did she get in with him
>
> So did she make the decision out of
>
> So did her split second decision come out of years of training, to be considerate, to think of others, to be, crucially enough, a good girl?[1]

It is remarkable just how faithful aspects of *The Good Parents* are to these first thoughts, a circumstance that might be accounted for, perhaps, by London having had these ideas for even longer. In her archive, two small pieces of rectangular brown paper dated from 1998, that is, during the drafting of *Gilgamesh* (2001), both have 'GP' written in the top left-hand corner, with the later one, from early August, containing only the portending lines 'They were good parents. They were. Good parents'.[2] It would be ten years later that the novel of that name would be published.

London has noted that one of her motivations for writing *The Good Parents* was 'to explore—or present—a time of idealism that was part of my particular generation. That terrible thing of trying to live in communes".[3] It was an idea (and lived experience) that seems to have preoccupied London for quite a while. In a talk she gave at Warana Writers's Week in 1987, she told her audience:

> I came of age in the sixties ... The particular path I took led me to living in a shack in the hills outside Perth for a year, and then in a farmhouse in a country town. This was regarded as a sort of apprenticeship to living on the land, communally, completely away from decadent society. The word was 'self-sufficient'. I remember heated debates as to whether this was opting out or whether it was 'the only alternative'. The idea of it, if not the reality, captured my imagination for about four years.
>
> Of course, there are many reasons as to why a part of a generation should start reading Krishnamurti, and form a small movement 'back to the land'. I think of it an offshoot of, another form of puritanism, searching for a new land,

a new frontier. Although it was germinated through reading, it was not conducive to writing or reading, apart from the Vedantas[ara] or Herman Hesse. The main idea in those early flag-waving days was 'Be. Don't think'. I dismissed writing as a 'head trip', an irrelevancy, an 'ego trip'. All the same, I took notes.

Also the role of women in this movement, if properly carried through—I never got that far—seemed almost Biblical, toiling on the land, spinning wool, baking bread. There wouldn't be much time for writing.

...

In the middle of all of this, I remember very clearly driving one night from our shack to visit some friends in their shack. [On the car radio] I heard the beautiful measured tones of an American [John Updike] talking about why he wrote fiction.

...

His talk electrified me.

...

Eventually I came to write my first story. This was after my own true urban nature had reasserted itself and with great thankfulness I was back living in the city.[4]

London can assume that many of *The Good Parents*' readers living in the early twenty-first century will most likely have a shared, burnished image, if not experience, of this sixties generation—free love, dope, sandals, beads, lentils, radical politics—to which her main characters in *The Good Parents* belong and are reflecting on at some temporal distance. Yet, *The Good Parents* pushes through the clichés to contemplate what constitutes a good life by imagining this era's ripple effects across three generations. As conceptual tools, generations are particularly favoured by demographers and political scientists to organise and understand the social world, to bring the chaos of lives into order and knowability. In London's novel, they are fault lines in families that necessitate a narrative attentiveness to messiness and ambivalence, and they afford consideration of the responsibilities parents and children have to each other. In this way, they also allow the novel its explorations of, rather than solutions to, the quest to 'be' and so afford its characters a recognition of the limits to knowing others.

The novel's main narrative takes place some decades following the heyday of the sixties, over a couple of wintry months in the year 2000. Occasional references to the upcoming Olympics and, at the novel's near conclusion, the Essendon football team's Grand Final win against the Melbourne Demons, secures the novel in this specific historical moment and the novel's sense of realism. Toni and Jacob de Jong are (some of) the parents to whom the book's title refers; they are also recalled as children of 'parents who had grown up in the Depression and set up house after the war' (253), suggesting that one of London's interests for this novel is to think about how families shape their members and set them on course for differing, and repeating, life trajectories. By their own daughter, they are dismissively regarded as 'old hippies', but they have other ideas about themselves: 'They both wore jeans and worn leather jackets, and much-polished R.M. Williams boots, more like aging rockers than hippies' (44).[5] As is repeatedly commented upon, Toni is a notable beauty 'with movie star looks' (229); Jacob is a high school English teacher; and they live together with their son Magnus and, until recently, their daughter Maya in the (fictional) Western Australian wheatbelt town of Warton.

Just graduated from secondary school herself, eighteen-year-old Maya has travelled to Melbourne to find work (and to put distance between herself and an impermissible sexual encounter with a young believer of the Brethren faith), but she has not been seen by her film-maker housemate, Cecile, for some days. With their arrival in Melbourne to spend a planned three months with their daughter, Toni and Jacob introduce into the narrative the idea that Maya has disappeared. The rest of the book turns on their hopeful anticipation that she will make contact and weaves together the memories and experiences of Toni and Jacob, as well as many others whose lives have overlapped with theirs, that emerge from their state of waiting.

As such, the title of *The Good Parents* is a potentially misleading entry point into this world and its preoccupations. While parents are certainly present—Toni and Jacob are central to the narrative—they are part of London's signature ensemble of characters whose intersecting experiences, memories and behaviours that comprise the story are difficult to describe as 'good'. This challenge arises not so much because London's characters exhibit traits that are other than 'good' but because what 'good' is or does is subtly probed rather than adjudicated. *The Good Parents* is a novel in which not a lot happens in terms of action or plot. Instead, the story is meditative and structured around montage and recurring motifs, some lifted from cinema, to yoke together characters who are otherwise emotionally, temporally, or physically distant. Some way into the novel, Toni ruefully admits, 'I want to be honourable. I want to be *good*' (241), but London's novel gently refuses to realise this desire easily. With the authorial voice quietened, the narrative point of view of *The Good Parents* shifts between the focalised perspectives of its characters to produce a complexly composite and arguably unresolved querying into family and intimate relationships.

Such irresolution is hardly satisfactory for the narrative forms from which *The Good Parents* would seem, at first blush, to take its cue: melodramatic and the detective-mystery genre. The narrative begins somewhat unconventionally: postcoital, Maya is pictured performing her toiletry while contemplating in cinematic close-up the women's bathroom of her workplace: 'There was a quicklime incinerator for tampons … rotating chrome soap dispensers, the mint-green handbasins on their pedestals, the big wire basket for paper towels' (1). But very soon after this intriguing introduction, the novel moves into familiar narrative territory: melodrama. Throughout its history, emerging in the eighteenth century, melodrama has been associated with sensationalism, Manichean conflict, stock characters—villainous types and virtuous maidens, for example—and malevolent intrigue. Maya is purposefully not presented as 'virtuous' in any nineteenth-century sense, but she is bundled out of the narrative at the end of the first chapter in a way that recalls a lurid conclusion of an act in a melodramatic play. Maya and her boss Maynard Flynn, along with a creepily voyeuristic Mr. T, Flynn's business partner who is pictured spying on the couple's foreplay, are depicted leaving the office in the conclusion of the first chapter, although the terms of this departure are no more explicable for having been shown. London carefully and ambiguously represents their exit as not an instance of clear abduction—'Her legs went one after the other as if they didn't belong to her anymore' (39)—but neither is it entirely non-coercive. London leans on the devices of melodrama but confuses the moral certainty they are conventionally asked to uphold. In so doing, she introduces into the text the ambivalences and ambiguities that arise in her exploration of her characters' internal lives and their outward expressions and entanglements. Further, in an instance of dramatic irony, London's readers are made aware of this happening in a way that Maya's parents, Toni and Jacob, are not.

At first, when she does not appear as arranged, her parents agree that 'Maya wished no one to worry, she wished to be left alone. They must respect that' (51). But soon enough they are calling 'the Missing Persons Bureau' (56), which would seem to be leading *The Good Parents* and its readers towards the conventions of the crime genre. Jacob helps this idea along by relaying to Cecile, in his initial confusion as to his daughter's whereabouts and seemingly oblivious to Cecile's own claims to film knowledge given her profession, 'Right now I feel as if I'm in a film myself … A mystery. A crime thriller? Most plots turn around a crime these days, have you noticed? It's become the norm' (50). And yet London quickly dispenses with that possibility. The staff at the Bureau are largely disinterested and are perhaps even suspicious of a father making enquiries into the movements of his daughter, who is a young adult, after all, and may well have her own reasons to refuse communication. This rebuff leaves Toni and Jacob with the provoking knowledge that 'their daughter was missing, whatever that meant. She was out of their reach' (56). To them, Maya's disappearance is both a material fact and an existential turning point: in the face of their daughter's absence, Toni and Jacob's limits as parents, the fragility of their marriage, and their daughter's claims to independent adulthood, are painfully revealed to them.

London foregrounds an interest in this family dynamic early in the novel by means of a passage of dialogue between Toni and Jacob initially puzzling over Maya's 'disappearance'. London writes:

> 'It isn't like her,' Jacob said.
>
> 'Isn't it? You know how we get on her nerves.'
>
> 'That's because we still matter to her. She's very loyal, really. She's never let us down before.'
>
> 'Remember how I treated my parents?'
>
> 'We're not parents like your parents.' Right from the start, this had been an article of faith between them.
>
> 'Maybe we are to Maya.'
>
> ...
>
> 'Maybe this is her way of telling us that she wants to be left alone in her new life.'
>
> 'Maybe it isn't anything to do with us. Most likely she got the date wrong and she'll be back tomorrow.' (47)

This image of parents worrying about the whereabouts of their (adult) child, marking out their differences from their own parents, and entertaining the ways in which their daughter might feel about them, is the hinge of *The Good Parents* as much as Maya's absence is. And if Maya's disappearance is not a missing person case to be solved by the usual storylines, then other narratives forms that afford different ways of knowing are necessary for London's novel. Toni suggests as much about half-way through the narrative in the knowledge that Maya has telephoned her brother Magnus in Warton:

> It wasn't a death after all. It wasn't an abduction. Not even a missing person case, since Maya couldn't quite give up

> Magnus. But now, as clearly as if she were watching through Mimi's glass door [of the beauty salon adjacent to Maya's office], Toni saw Maya pass down the dingy hallway, her head bowed, following two men. (182)

The story that unfolds from Maya's presumed disappearance, and which turns on a repertoire of images—of light and reflection, for instance, as well as mirrors—and a patterning of chapters that loop in time rather than unfurl linearly, is therefore significantly distinct from the sleuthing and clue-gathering that any Missing Persons Bureau plot-driven account would presumably set in train. Clearly the novel begins on a dramatic note; or, rather, the crisis is recognised as such once Maya's parents determine that their daughter is missing. But, the novel's framing narrative, which centres largely on Toni's and Jacob's responses to their daughter's disappearance, or claims to independence, gives rise to the memories, hopes and regrets that formally structure the novel.

As an example, and given what has come sequentially before—Maya's leaving with Flynn, and Toni and Jacob discovering that their daughter is 'missing'—the novel might be expected to offer knowledge of what follows Maya's departure. Instead, the reader is presented with a change in place and a rupture in time. The narrative shifts to tell of Toni's own leaving—of childhood, of middle-class life, much like Maya—in the terms that London initially set out for herself in her fresh notebook and which are familiar to the gothic fairytale:

> Once in a spring twilight, a schoolgirl was waiting for a bus on the edge of the highway between Fremantle and Perth when a stranger in a low black car pulled up and offered her

> a lift. And without a word, against a lifetime's warnings, the girl, Toni Parker, climbed in (58).

The break in time and space, from Melbourne in 2000 to Perth in the late 1960s, introduces the novel's many-layered and overlapping storylines. It also makes readers aware of how this novel is to be patterned: interdependent presents and pasts are made adjacent at the same time that the narrative unfolds chronologically, from the moment of Maya's leaving at the novel's beginning to her return to an empty house at the end with assistance, as it happens, from this same stranger in the low black car.

London's opening chapters introduce the main characters; the suggestion that their lives are separate and interwoven; and the idea that each character's inner life and histories will surface by way of accretion. They also put in place the principles of cinematic montage on which the novel turns. While not emblematic in terms of summarising the novel's fictional reality—the usual metonymic job given to the beginning shot in narrative cinema—nor indeed an establishing wide-shot (the oftentimes preferred starting point for standard cinema), the way London introduces Maya in the novel's first chapter is expressly filmic. Even before she is established as a character, with a face and a body to prepare for the day ahead and an inner life that worries at the flowers she has purchased in tribute to her lover-boss's recently deceased wife—another of the novel's many related storylines—the novel represents Maya as an almost incorporeal, observing filmic consciousness. The first lines of the novel read:

> The best time was always afterwards, alone, in the Ladies' Restroom on the first floor. It had high frosted-glass window

> that at this hour, before the frail winter sun had found its way between the buildings of the city, shed a grainy light like old footage in a documentary film. (1)

This vision, together with her extended surveying of the bathroom, presents Maya as a kind of subjective camera, recording her surrounds and wondering 'How long since this room had been modernised?' (1) Throughout the story from this point, the characters make passing reference to aspects of cinema and so they are conjoined in ways they themselves do not immediately recognise. Magnus, Maya's brother, imagines a future visual project that also resonates with the novel's formal and thematic concerns:

> He had an idea for a video clip called *Six Thousand and One Nights in Warton*. That was about how long he would have spent here—his whole life—when he left. Everything would go into it one day. Samples of old film themes, car horns, road trains, barking dogs, show day. Crows, crickets, the school bell, the radio in the Lucky [Warton's drive-in cinema], all the background static that you didn't notice anymore. Bits of music that his father used to play and his photos of the drive-in. The sound of bike tyres over gravel. Everything flowing together, flowing forward. (142)

If their children oftentimes conceive of the world cinematically, Toni and Jacob themselves are repeatedly cast in film terms. They are described as 'a sort of small-town version of Nick Nolte and Anjelica Huston' (44), for instance, and later in the narrative, but earlier in time, Toni's physical appearance prompts comparisons with film stars such as 'Elizabeth Hurley' (224) and 'Natalie Wood' (83). Jacob, too, is aligned with cinema: he is a secretly failed scriptwriter who romanticises his youth as 'vaguely French New Wave' (96)—presumably low budget and with the sense of spontaneity jump cuts afford—and this stalled ambition frames his vision and memory. On smoking his first joint as a teenager, he sees that 'The sky had turned a cinematic purple and he started to feel he was in a film' (63). London has Toni share her husband's filmic repertoire even as they are pictured drifting apart in middle-age. Privately, and tellingly, Toni recollects her former life married to Cy Fisher, the stranger in the black car who comes to control her life and then finds her adult daughter, in a specifically cinematic way: 'a silent movie. She couldn't remember the words' (273).

This passing reference to silent cinema not only suggests how Fisher continues to replay in Toni's memory. it also returns to the novel's interest in melodrama and subtly acknowledges the role Fisher has in it: in an early description of Fisher, his 'five o'clock shadow' is theatrically, and knowingly, nominated as 'villainous' (79). Without speech, silent movies enthusiastically embraced the theatricality of melodrama; Toni's imagining of Fisher in such terms helps to make sense of the way in which he both is linked in the novel with the implausible events that characterise melodrama and, to some extent, moves along what there is of a plot in *The Good Parents*. Toni half-recognises this role of Fisher when she admits to herself that '[h]e was the reason for everything, Jacob, their children, the way they lived' (330). Toni is reflecting here on how her earlier life with Fisher has given shape to what has followed, but she could just as easily be thinking about his importance for the novel's narrative design and rhythm. Fisher, after all, emerges out of nowhere—as he does throughout the novel—on a rainy afternoon and changes the trajectory of young Toni's middle-class life; his wholly improbable encounter with an older Toni in the crowds at the Melbourne football grand final leads to his 'discovery' of Maya and his return of her to Melbourne.

But if reference to film from the first page sets the novel's watchful posture, its purposeful pace, and its montage aesthetic, then it is one aspect of cinema—light—that London almost imperceptibly refers to for both dramatic and realist effect. London's touch in this regard is very gentle as befits the immateriality of her subject. Light filters across the novel from the 1970s Perth nightclub Toni frequents with Fisher—'From small windows near the ceiling the summer twilight fell in beams across the swept wooden floors' (80)—to Magnus's Warton contemporary bedroom—'A beam of light from the setting sun came over the paddocks, through the pine trees and the window of his room, straight onto the strained shining face of Miles Davis on his trumpet in the poster on the opposite wall' (101). London turns to light to describe Toni's nascent feelings for Jacob when he shows up, then unknown to her, to paint the Perth inner-city apartment she shares with Fisher: 'The late sun caught on the silver Sikh's bangle on his thin brown arm. She thought of the word *light* when she saw him' (184). Years later, but only a handful of pages subsequently, Jacob repeats, with a twist, the same phrase but with reference instead to his daughter's housemate, Celeste: 'What was the expression? She was *light on the eye*' (215). The patterning of light in this latter instance connects Toni and Jacob, and also underscores their mounting emotional distance. At other moments in the narrative, key or hard lighting draws attention to another of the novel's immaterial preoccupations, which is nevertheless keenly felt: time. When smoking a joint outside at night with Dieter, Celeste's business partner, London's referencing of artificial illumination emphasises a conflict Jacob finds himself inadvertently getting into:

> He looked up to the sky above the courtyard. 'You can hardly see the stars in Melbourne.'
>
> Dieter made a barking noise. 'You guys are so cosmic with your drugs.'
>
> 'What do you mean "you guys"?'
>
> 'Your generation. *The Doors of Perception*. Did you read that? …
>
> 'Why do you smoke then?' In the spotlight over the fishpond he could see that Dieter was well into his thirties, a Generation X-er, a natural enemy. (160)

In addition to emphasising generational difference, the spotlight also illuminates time. Time is a major concern for the novel not simply because it is inevitably passing—the novel tells of Toni's and Jacob's early years alongside their young adult lives and as parents of late-teenage children—and because the novel rests on apparent generational distinctions, as Jacob's encounter with Dieter suggests. It is also of interest because of the significance attributed to the pause on which the novel hinges. Toni and Jacob are waiting for Maya to call; both are relatively stilled in their own way—Jacob ends up with a broken foot so is physically immobilised and Toni signs up to a Buddhist retreat—but the world around them seems to be on the cusp of an anticipated future, which promises to usher in some uncertain form of radical newness.

It is not incidental that *The Good Parents* is set at the turn of the millennium, a temporal marker that, however illogical, is somehow momentous and epoch-defining. (It will be remembered by many of London's readers that the Y2K bug threatened to collapse computer infrastructure and, by extension, the so-called developed world). In the novel, apocalyptic anxiety is felt keenly by Warton's Brethren community, which anticipates the great flood; the premonition of a geological quake sees property developers buy up land with little thought to those people who live displaced at the 'swampy parts of the river with the few desolate Aboriginal cottages' (209). Alongside this heightened apprehension, the augured novelty of that time, and the generational difference that the passing of time produces, is represented in London's book by Toni and Jacob's attitudes towards technology. Without a thought, Cecile edits films on her laptop and Dieter casually watches 'porn on the internet' (160), yet Toni buys her first mobile phone while in Melbourne with the aside that 'Magnus would be pleased with this purchase' (111), which suggests the uniqueness of the occasion. While Toni's acquisition is given a passing glance in the narrative, London affords Jacob a much longer passage that has him identify and reflect on technological change and impresses some sense of the edge of time:

> Something new was happening. He felt as if he'd woken up from a pastoral dream and the world had changed. It was in the grip of ceaseless, relentless electronic innovation and it was just beginning. It seems to Jacob that they were on the verge of a social revolution as great as that of his own generation in the sixties. It was no longer possible to ignore it even in Warton. When they returned and gave Magnus his computer, their life would change. Non-stop communication and information. (116)

Reading this passage now, close to twenty-five years on from its historical setting, it is tempting to praise Jacob as a seer while quelling the impossible desire to travel back in time to let him know that apps, ChatGPT, 3-D printing and virtual reality headsets are just around the corner.[6] But Jacob's observations here extend beyond what he perceives as a changing time. He also imagines his experience up to that point in literary terms that suggest an idyll existing outside of historical time. His reference to the pastoral—an imaginary world of simple, idealised rural life that sees love and song, rather than labour, as diverting shepherds and shepherdesses—might seem apt, even excusable, given that Jacob is an English teacher with a head full of Leo Tolstoy and lines from John Milton's *Paradise Lost*. But it also registers a thematic concern of *The Good Parents* that Jacob only half-articulates at this moment: a querying of idealism less as a systematic theory—Jacob is not immersed in the thinking of the eighteenth-century idealist philosopher Emmanuel Kant—and more as an everyday tussling with what a good and meaningful life might look like in the twenty-first century.

Closer to the story's end, for example, Jacob is pictured walking through the Melbourne streets, his foot now recovered but his mind restless; he has just emerged from a frustrating interview about Maya's potential whereabouts with a man he distrusts. In illuminating cinematic fashion, 'A solitary nineteenth-century street lamp came suddenly alight' and, appropriately enough given the dated light source, Jacob is thrown into memories of childhood that lead into somewhat despairing ruminations on his life course:

> Ideology. All his primal energy, his youthful virility had gone into an idealistic movement that had simply petered

> out, been subsumed by new imperatives, by the world grinding on. The great wave of his times had swept him up and dumped him in a country town, left him stranded, washed-up, a dinosaur. No wonder his kids wanted to get away as soon as possible. (285)

Here history is conceived of as an inexorable natural force and, in the face of it, Jacob's sense of self-defeat is palpable, with the metaphors Jacob leans on implicitly segueing into thoughts about his own father, unknown and presumed drowned at sea but for whom Jacob has always carried a suspicion, or perhaps even a hope, of an afterlife elsewhere. But the novel does not build to such a moment as an instance of self-revelation. Instead, this refrain—a sense of an unmet idealism worn down by abstract forces that are nevertheless profoundly felt—is one to which Jacob returns. As London has Jacob reflect a little earlier in the novel:

> Gradually he'd stopped thinking of himself as a revolutionary in exile. The revolution hadn't happened, instead there was *economic rationalism*. The movement he belonged to, so careless and playful and ragged, had barely lasted ten years. Its gurus were discredited. A gear-change in history had swallowed it up. (216)

But *The Good Parents* declines to rest conclusively on the pessimistic note it attributes to Jacob. Long passages of the novel are given over to Jacob's and Toni's memories of that 'idealist movement', which comes to define and differentiate them and their generation, and which might also be read as circling around ideas of authenticity as elements of goodness that the novel comes quietly to value.

Some of Jacob's most substantial thoughts about his past arise in the novel's present time, when he accidentally locks himself out of the Melbourne share house and finds himself stoned and stranded on a small balcony in cold weather. In this situation, once again forcibly stationary, he recalls discussions with Toni about 'the great adventure, the last frontier ... a different way of life' (228) and her eventual decision to leave Fisher and join him in 'monastic-style rituals, harmony with nature, mystical things ... an elite network that would eventually have its own schools, and bands and poetry, its own trading arrangements' (228–9). While Jacob is physically trapped, the tumbling nature of his words suggests the movement of his mind and the energy generated by his earlier aspirations; these are only halted by the welcome appearance of Cecile and her promise of rescue, inverting the somewhat begrudging image Jacob has of himself in his mental narrative as Toni's 'knight errant' (238), liberating her from Fisher and his gangster style of living.

In accordance with the novel's cinematic principle of montage, the next chapter titled 'Karma' centres on Toni, who has turned to Buddhism 'in her current state of uncertainty and worry' (246) and in the hope of achieving something transcendent of the self. Jacob seems to have once shared Toni's yearning, with London writing of him in the preceding chapter:

> Beneath the surface of his life lay a substructure of belief, long neglected but never quite forgotten, like the music from adolescence, an ideology made up of bits of Eastern religions and the theories of his youth. A spiritual quest that he still turned to for consolation, but which he no longer believed had the power to change the world. It contained the secret hope that through the simple life you could become

> enlightened. That something numinous was waiting at the end of the road. (216)

London's characters are untroubled by what might be viewed as their selective or even appropriative faith, although London's use here of the word 'bits' suggests a gentle critique of her characters' assumption to pick and choose religious beliefs that has, perhaps, more in common with the logic of capitalism than Jacob would like to admit. That the key to Maya's house is kept hidden beneath a Buddha statue near the fishpond similarly suggests capitalism's remit to transform the sacred into kitsch, one aspect of the twenty-first-century world London's characters are inhabiting that nevertheless holds faint traces of other, persistent values; in the last pages of the novel Toni is pictured as alert to such signs, wondering at 'a row of ragged Tibetan flags waving … Decoration, or a frail reminder of the spirit' (346).

Yet, these ideals are subject to scrutiny. In *The Good Parents*, 'Karma' does not refer expressly to the religious belief in the future effects of present actions, although it does unavoidably carry that resonance for both Toni and Jacob, and presumably London's readers, too. But most obviously for London's novel, 'Karma' refers to a remembered commune in south-west Western Australia that Toni and Jacob joined, and whose naming as such strikes even them as painfully obvious. Toni recalls her experience at the commune without fondness: 'She could hardly face the relentless beans and rice' (257). But perhaps more tellingly, her memories of that time intersect with those of Jacob on the point of their individual truthfulness, or lack thereof. Jacob's recall of Toni and their commune experiment is of her looking 'like a hippy or a gypsy, but in fact, he reflected bitterly, she was anything but' (239) and Toni returns the criticism in a way that recalls to a reader's mind her husband's physical and existential predicament on the balcony in the preceding chapter:

> Already she knew more about Jacob than she ever had about Cy. She noticed how he changed … using the right language, 'man' and 'trippy' and 'bummer'. To hear him you would think he had no personal past, no experiences that weren't political or psychedelic. He reinvented himself as one of the new breed.
>
> It hurt her somehow, the way he changed. To see him as the outsider, trying to get in. (257)

The adjustments in speech and dress that both characters self-consciously adopt to meet the vision of their idealism is presented by London as forced and inauthentic. And these external modifications are counterposed in the novel with inner shifts that Toni and Jacob barely perceive in their present time but to which a reader is subtly alerted by the novel's repeated return to multiple ruminations on 'goodness'. London's novel is not unsympathetic towards Toni and Jacob, who find themselves in changing times and carrying an abiding quest for spiritual meaningfulness. But *The Good Parents* does give pause to what are presented as the realities of their unquestioning idealism. And in place of any final revelation 'at the end of the road', the novel instead forwards, and enacts, small changes as constituting at least part of what 'good' could entail.

London herself has referred obliquely to this aspect of the novel:

> Well I think change is complex. We don't always change the way we think we have. Sometimes you realise that you have

> changed, but maybe it's not something very dramatic. I love it, actually. I love, personally, feeling that I've opened up in an area where I might have shut a door. There's nothing I like more. And nothing I respect more in people than to see them open and change. How wonderful it is, when you're young, to see older people who come around, and understand why you're doing something your way. When I see that happening now, I think: Bravo! Because that's what life is, really. Changing and opening, if you can. It's very hard, to yield or give up something you might have hung your hat on for so long.[7]

The final chapters of *The Good Parents* see Toni come to a small realisation on which the novel centres: 'It occurred to her that for all these years what she'd called "good" was no more than fear and guilt and prudence ... She still didn't know what "good" was' (346). That Toni has these thoughts in the company of Fisher, many years after their separation, is meaningful. Fisher had proclaimed to the younger Toni with resolute determination that he would not become a father and he is arguably the least variable character in London's novel: he does not seem to have doubts. Admittedly, little is given of his internal life, but what a reader does come to know of Fisher is consistent throughout. When Toni encounters him years later, he looks 'trimmer and more youthful looking than he used to be' (328) but she also intuits that 'there would always be business' and '[h]e would never retire' (329, 330). As a figure filched from melodrama, assured of his part, he is equipped to 'find' Maya in a way that her parents cannot, not least because they are unsure about their own roles, a point underscored by Jacob's expressed concern that 'he didn't really know how to be a father, not having grown up with one' (114). Fisher's own drunkard father is also absent—he is said to have died when he is a teenager—but Fisher's refrain, 'You never look back. That way there was never any fuss' (121) suggests a way of being that is not shared by Jacob or Toni. While admitted by London's narrative, Fisher's method of moving through the world is called into question by both the ways in which the narrative structure of *The Good Parents* returns to the past and the hesitant future the novel imagines.

As London writes in relation to Jacob, for example, 'As he opened the front door he felt a pang of sadness, as if, by getting on with their lives, he and Toni were moving further away from Maya. Who knows? he thought … perhaps she needed us to change' (217). Rather than the external changes that both Toni and Jacob decry in each other, it is this inner shift, marked by hesitation, that the novel approves of for its characters. In their own way, all of London's characters are guided, or stymied, by the humanist injunction to 'know thyself', whether it be hoped for by time spent at Karma; sensed by the 'pull to the horizon' that Magnus feels in Warton (143); or Jacob's reading of Tolstoy 'with his [the author's] "problem of the self"' (162). Even Fisher, the least metaphysically inclined of London's characters, sees himself as part of something larger. As he tells Maya: 'Someone looks after me, no doubt about it. I've got a first-rate guardian angel' (348). But it is a querying that occurs alongside Jacob's rescripting of the maxim 'know thyself' that admits doubt.

Jacob's rhetorical questioning—'Who knows?'—is marked by further uncertainty that a reader is asked to note because of his additional use of the word 'perhaps'. Jacob's apparent indecision, in its narrative context, is not prevarication but rather a productive doubt carrying both hesitation and possibility. Jacob no longer assumes to know what his daughter needs or wants.

Instead, his rumination is a recognition of Maya as an individual young woman to whom, as her father, he is also very much emotionally tied. And it is perhaps this quality that Andy Flynn implicitly recognises in Jacob when he tells Maya, before she is met by Fisher at the novel's near-end, that '*Your* father came to see me last week. I don't think he trusted me, but he seemed like a good guy' (336). Towards his own father, Maynard Flynn—Maya's problematic, controlling lover and boss who theatrically bundled her out of the office and first chapter—Andy has other, ambivalent feelings that not only cast Jacob positively but also implicate Maya and point to the tangled, at times manipulative, emotional lives of London's characters which constitute *The Good Parents*: 'He wants you to hate him, Maya. He hates himself so much. You shouldn't be loyal to him, it will only make it worse' (336). Relationships between children and parents, and lovers, are far from straightforward in London's novel. Unlike Jacob, however, Maynard Flynn's inner life is narratively negligible, so self-revelation is withheld from him. Yet, his son's apprehension points to the possibility of psychological complexity that belies the initial melodramatic image the novel presents of Maynard, villainously spiriting Maya away and which repeats, in its way, Fisher's coaxing (a reader today might even say grooming) of Toni away from her conventional family life decades before.

This repetition of actions or behaviours across the generations is underscored by the novel's motif of the mirror. This image suggests not so much that children will necessarily, for better and for worse, rehearse the lives, scripts and traumas of their parents, although it is true those ideas are certainly possible to take from *The Good Parents*. Instead, like the dispersal of light that distinguishes this novel and the cinematic references that it entertains, the understated recurrence of mirrors throughout London's pages draws contemplative attention to the self and relations with others that the generations, with their differences, are asked to share.

Mirrors, of course, have complex philosophical and material histories and have been put to various symbolic and literary purposes: they play out the dialectic of appearance and essence; they reflect, distort and reveal the self (as vain, as deceived, as present) as well as promise access to knowledge that is variously divine, artistic and secular. In London's novel, mirrors most often provide a moment's pause of self-reflection, which is directed towards observing physical change (and the passing of time) as much as existential querying.

Among many instances, the very last page of *The Good Parents* has Maya looking into the bathroom mirror and seeing that her face 'was thinner, paler, almost translucent' (349), a gesture that echoes the novel's opening bathroom sequence in which she features and which is also a scene of memory and (dis)identification: 'Every morning at this mirror she thought for a moment of her mother and the compulsive little pout she made when she looked at herself, like an old-fashioned model' (2). Later, Maya vaguely recalls going to a drunken party with Maynard and entering a 'lift with a dim mirror reflecting the two of them going up, side by side, no touching, like a father and a daughter' (334), the mirror a mute witness to what they do not articulate.

Elsewhere in the novel, Jacob and his sister, Kitty, are recalled studying 'themselves in mirrors' that their dressmaker mother uses (68), a playful interest in the self, and Jacob is pictured subsequently turning to mirrors to scrutinise himself and others. His first (envy-tinged) assessment of the generation X-er Dieter is that his hair is as if 'he'd attacked it himself in front of a mirror' (153); later, he turns his gaze onto himself and determines that in the mirror 'his eyes looked different to him' (165). In Melbourne, Jacob looks again to the mirror to see his face 'paler than it had been in Warton, and there was a new, sad puffiness under his eyes' (217) and once more to notice 'his jaw sagging, his gut loosening, his hands turning red and knobbly' at a moment in which he wonders at his (unreciprocated) desire for his daughter's housemate, Cecile (288).

For her part, Toni also looks to mirrors repeatedly. As she searches for 'clues' to Maya's disappearance, she finds herself in her daughter's workplace bathroom. What she observes there, however, is not the self-admiring lip-puckering image of another's desire, as her daughter had projected, but rather that 'shadows fall across her face' (179). Toni makes a point of expressly noting the absence of mirrors in the Buddhist ashram, too, and at an earlier time but later in the novel, she thinks of herself as 'too vivid for the mirror' she encounters at her family home after some months at Karma (261). In this encounter, there is a sense of the image's limit; the represented self cannot contain the experienced self. Towards the end of the novel, Toni views herself in the mirror once again, this time at the football stadium's bathroom. Her head having been recently shaved at the ashram, Toni sees in the mirror, 'herself at last … her whole face carved into a new angularity' (327). Yet at the same time, and much as the mirror gave rise for Maya a vision of her mother, Toni's self-revelation is imbricated in the image-memory of her own mother: 'She caught a glimpse, like a ghost, of the hawkish features of Beryl' (327). Haunted in this way, Toni then immediately steps outside and unexpectedly finds herself 'face to face with Cy Fisher' (327), another kind of mirroring that surfaces forgotten feelings, 'the old luxurious pull of relinquishment to him ... Though she rarely thought of him now, she sometimes still had dreams of him ... and she woke feeling tender towards him' (330). Earlier in their lives, on the run from Fisher, Toni and Jacob 'saw their faces in the tarnished mirror over the bar, small and smudged like newsprint' (231); later, when Toni confronts Fisher about her decision to leave him, the two are pictured looking 'at one another via the mirror behind the bar' (268), with the mirror as mediator and the image it affords confirmation of their separation.

The mirror, like London's patterning of light and cinematic references, suggest the novel's concern to imagine subjectivity and experience as refracted, dispersed but also constituted across multiple moments, times and relationships. As such, *The Good Parents* makes its own contribution to a long literary tradition that grapples with what Jacob nominates 'the problem of the self'. Yet, unlike Jacob's beloved Tolstoy to whom Jacob attributes that enquiry and who surveyed the (Russian) human condition, offering counsel for its correct course, London's novel leaves what is good unresolved. The effect is not one of indifference or moral relativity, but rather a sense that questions of goodness are open-ended and all-the-more compelling and important to represent and contemplate for this unanswerability.

The Golden Age

At some point in her short visit to Perth as part of the 1954 Royal Tour, of which Joan London's *The Golden Age* (2014) tells in brief, Queen Elizabeth II is presented with bouquets that 'had been placed, untouched, onto a table for Her Majesty to inspect'.[1] One of those floral arrangements finds its way to the Golden Age, a children's polio convalescent home, where everybody 'took photos of it, or cut pieces of the ribbon as mementos' (153). In the novel, these are small, even incidental, scenes. After all, *The Golden Age* is a novel that predominantly focuses on a Jewish Hungarian family repairing a post-Holocaust life in the small capital city of Western Australia, and centres on the experience of Ferenc/Frank, the only child of Ida and Meyer Gold, who is undergoing rehabilitation at the Golden Age hospice having contracted polio. And yet, the bouquet, both distanced and proximate, unexpectedly suggests the shifting affective, temporal and physical relations that *The Golden Age* has its characters negotiate as it tells of Frank's coming of age as a poet. And it is also a call to attend to, and value, the otherwise unremarkable; to be alive 'to a world where everything had meaning' (238), as

Frank writes in a preface to a book that honours his first poetic mentor and captures the novel's abiding interest and significance.

As the Queen's fleeting appearance in the novel suggests, part of *The Golden Age*'s world is grounded in what might be termed 'reality' or 'history'. The Queen did indeed visit Perth in 1954 as part of her 58-day Australian tour, which saw her start her journey by arriving in Sydney Harbour on the *SS Gothic* to festooned streets and enormous fanfare, a reception that was repeated at every step of her excursion. What is also true is that there was a poliomyelitis epidemic at the time of her visit, which was known to cause permanent paralysis, especially in children, and sometimes death.

Historians have noted that from the emergence of the disease in Western Australia in 1938, three epidemics were identified and experienced—in 1948, 1954 and 1956—with Jonas Salk's successful development of a polio vaccine leading to radical reductions in incidents of the disease worldwide.[2] In this context, the telling of the Queen's short time in Perth in London's novel not only gives rise to a gently humorous recognition of monarchical sentiment in Australia, but also a querying as to whose lives might be remembered and valued: 'The Queen survived Western Australian unaffected … A week or two after the *Gothic* sailed off across the Indian Ocean, however, half a dozen new cases of polio were reported, contracted amongst the crowds gathered at the roadsides to see her' (153). This asking takes on further urgency and force given that the family members central to London's story are refugees, sorrowfully aware of the lives of others extinguished, and part of the postwar 'migration' that restructured not only Australian society but also the world order, and which did not always generate the hospitality the Queen and her entourage enjoyed.

Furthermore, this telling of the Queen's visit has the purpose of supporting how the story presents itself from its near beginning; as a historical novel of sorts, inviting its readers into an awareness of its factual coordinates. As London writes of the place that gives her book both its title and the name of the second section in which these details are relayed:

> 'The Golden Age' had been built as a pub at the turn of the century, in Leederville, five minutes' walk from the railway station, two stops out from the city centre. It stood alone, bounded by four flat roads, like an island, which in its present incarnation seemed to symbolise its apartness, a natural quarantine … The pub had been bought by the Health Department in 1949 and converted into the Golden Age Children's Polio Convalescent Home, to service the years of the great epidemics. Inside, with its ramps and bars and walkways, its schoolteacher, trained nurses and full-time physiotherapist, it was a modern treatment centre, which could accommodate up to fourteen children, some from the country, some who could not be cared for at home … The name, inherited, could be considered tactless by some, even cruelly ironic. These children were impaired as no one could ever wish a child to be. But perhaps because of its former role, its solid and generous air, it was a cheerful place. The children were no longer sick, but in need of help to find their way back into the world. (6–7)

With this description, London signals that her novel is firmly situated in the material world, but one that also holds imaginative possibilities. The latter is even more necessary since the site of which London writes—an inner-city block bordered by Alfred Street, Harrogate Street and Cambridge Street—is now part of the seemingly ever-expanding freeway that connects the Perth city centre to satellite suburbs in the north. And the Golds' house 'in North Perth, two stops by train from the Golden Age and a mile's walk up Fitzgerald Street' would today be passed by thousands of commuters heading through the inner-city surburb into the central business district, should it exist (13). But, for an author of London's creative range, the appeal of the Golden Age, with its changing fortunes and unlikely, resonant, name, is wholly understandable. As London told an audience at the 2015 Adelaide Writers' Week in a year that saw *The Golden Age* awarded the Prime Minister's Literary Award for fiction, the Kibble Literary Award, the Western Australian Premier's Award for fiction and the Queensland Literary Award for fiction (and in terms that would become all too familiar as the Covid-19 pandemic emerged only a few years following that interview):

> I became interested in writing about polio; I wanted to write something about the fifties. The fifties made me think of being a little girl at school ... Then I had this memory of lining up; we all had to line up to be injected, to have the polio vaccination, which had just come in. Up until then, because I have older sisters, I knew that my mother had been terribly frightened about polio for my older sisters. It was a dreadful thing that would sweep in. It was called the summer plague. And, and, and nobody knew how the children got it. And they tried different things to... You know, you musn't swim in the river and you couldn't go to cinemas or anything like that. Everyone was so frightened about it. So, I started to research it in the local history museum in Perth and found that there

> had been this place called the Golden Age and I was intrigued by it. And I rather like things that are like an ensemble, like building up a little world with a list of characters who all interact with one another. So that was the beginning of it.[3]

London's novel is far from straightforward or simply 'something about the fifties'.[4] Helen Garner, the acclaimed Australian author who launched London's book in Melbourne, noted something similar:

> It all sounds so … simple and clear. Yet if we look more closely, if we pick apart the simple sentences, we find threads leading away in every direction, both openly and subliminally. … All our nerve ends are quivering. Our minds teem with questions, and our hearts are open to the answers that we sense will be provided, without haste, in the right order, and at the time that the owner of this enthralling voice decides is right.
>
> Joan London is a very quiet writer. She does not need to raise her voice, or to strive for effect. But out of all her books flows a powerful stream of that essential thing – authority. We recognize it at once, in the first few words, and we respond to it with our full attention. … There's always this wonderful narrative intelligence, this light, witty presence, holding us above the abyss.[5]

The novel's recreation of this particular place and time takes its cues from historical 'facts' but also has inventiveness as a vital resource, not least because its main character, Frank (Ferenc, as a child in Hungary), has poetic aspirations that are tied to the novel's own empathetic imagination.

If it is at all useful to begin to approach *The Golden Age* as a historical novel, then it might be equally advantageous to recognise its shared interests with the *Künstlerroman*, or a narrative that traces the development of the artist from childhood to maturity. Frank is apprenticed in the novel to a young man, Sullivan Backhouse, who had 'just turned eighteen' (25) and whose confinement to an iron lung sees him figuratively decollated, saintly: 'From the tank closest to the door a head protruded disembodied on its pillow like a head on a plate' (23). Up until the point of meeting Sullivan, Frank had 'hardly given poetry a moment's thought' (24). But as a secular prophet, whose roaming imagination is trapped in iron and is eventually stilled by disease, Sullivan's teachings are of the poetry Frank comes to want to write; the possibilities of free verse; and the vernacular that London's novel itself largely explores and represents: 'Poetry didn't have to be about heroics, Sullivan said. It didn't have to strut about. It could sound like someone speaking. It could be about personal things' (25).

Indeed, the novel ends with an image of Frank Gold in a homely New York office-study, a poet of some reputation who has recently published both a volume titled 'The Golden Age', 'a book of poems about children in a hospital recovering from polio' (238) and a posthumous book of poetry by Sullivan, long dead. Frank is being interviewed by a young would-be poet and magazine editor, who is the son of his first romantic love, Elsa Briggs. This conclusion carries the question as to whether what has just been read—the thirty-one chapter-vignettes (the thirty-second, 'New York', is unnumbered) that move across time unevenly rather than chronologically, and between characters—might be a narrative approximation of the older Frank's poetry collection. The final representation of him nevertheless seems to be a confirmation or realisation of Frank's artistic ambitions that Sullivan inspired. From a young age following his chance encounter with Sullivan, Frank intuits poetry—'Frank, staring from his pillows at the high dark window opposite, was engaged in composing a poem' (93)—and determines that writing will be his vocation.

Yet, insofar as the novel does telescope on the figure of the young, would-be artist, it certainly does not neatly follow the established conventions of the *Künstlerroman*. The novel has little interest in plot: Frank is not represented as struggling against careless parents and a philistine society that misunderstand his creative desires. Quite the opposite. Frank's father walks the streets of Perth and wonders 'if there's a poet growing up here somewhere' (143). And his mother is a renowned pianist who performed to great acclaim at the Liszt Ferenc Academy in Budapest before Jews were prohibited from playing.

Nor does the novel unfold a life that matures in a linear fashion. Instead, the novel is temporally tangled. The last section in New York takes place some decades after the penultimate scene, and the preceding narrative represents a relatively short time period—mostly the months Frank lives at the hospice—yet interweaves what is imagined as a formative period in an unexpected artistic life with the stories of others with whom Frank lives proximately. Like the black cockatoos that fly through the novel's skies and whose calls are heard differently—by the children at the Golden Age as homely and by Ida and Meyer Gold at their North Perth house as 'needing oiling' (14)—but which bring into narrative propinquity those at geographical and at times emotional, remove, the novel's patterning is meaningfully associative.

And so, and appropriately enough for a novel that turns on childhood, the fairytale is called on to play a specific role in London's narrative: London turns to this familiar literary genre to represent and understand Frank's circumstances at the Golden Age in her novel's first pages. For Frank, and as the initial page of the novel relates, his arrival at the hospice has him feeling 'like a pirate landing on an island of little maimed animals. A great wave had swept them up and dumped them here. All of them, like him, stranded and wanting to go home' (2). And this fairytale mode also provides a frame for both the relationship that develops between Frank and Elsa, a young girl near Frank's age who is a recovering patient, too, at the Golden Age, and the faint but enduring connection the two have as adults. Much later in life, Elsa and Frank are imagined as simultaneously inhabiting, at great distance in time and place, a fairytale-like 'tower' (235); Elsa's is built for her as an addition to her house near Cottesloe Beach where she can no longer walk due to the long-term effects of polio, and Frank's is his New York office, with its 'large bay window … that juts out one floor up over the sidewalk, with a view in both directions of the street' (234). These are resonant, architectural images of isolation that accord with both the social 'apartness' of the Golden Age where the two first meet and the magical register of the novel's first page, which introduces Elsa through Frank's observations and the conventions of the fairytale:

> One afternoon during rest time, the new boy, Frank Gold, left his bed, lowered himself into his wheelchair and glided down the corridor. … His first goal, as usual, was to set eyes on Elsa. He peered into Girls through the crack between the hinges of the half-opened door. He liked to see her face asleep. Even if her head was turned away into the pillow, the sight of her thick gold-brown plait somehow gave him

> hope. But this afternoon her bed was empty. … But where was Elsa? (1, 3)

Elsa here is admired by Frank as Sleeping Beauty and cast as Rapunzel; these tropes echo elsewhere in the novel, including the thoughts of Elsa's mother. Margaret Briggs turns to the language of fairytales to register not only the unexpectedness and rapidity of polio's bodily effects but also the singularity with which she lovingly attributes her daughter: 'The shock and violence of polio, the instant transformation of it, reminded her of a cruel trick, of sorcery in a fairytale. As if an evil monster had demanded the fairest in the land. Elsa was the sacrifice' (109). Tellingly, Elsa eludes Frank's storybook gaze; nor is she foregone as her mother fears as, despite her physical limitations, she practices medicine as an adult. And London is also careful to position Frank as not altogether beholden to his, and Margaret's, imagining of Elsa as surrendered and without agency. Rather, Frank's recourse to fairytales represents the references and workings of a child's mind. And as befits a child, Frank's thoughts are of sorcerous things—'It was if the whole place were under a spell. Only he had escaped …' (2) But his ruminations tellingly trail off, as the ellipses suggest, into another, more adult world, one that has Frank 'dying for a smoke … a resistance to the babyishness of this place, its pygmy toilets, its naps and rules, half-hospital, half-nursery school, and his feeling of demotion when he was sent there' (2). This desire is recognised by the offer of a light by Norm Whitehouse, the gardener, 'As if to say: a man has a right to smoke in peace' (3), with Whitehouse being the actual, fondly-remembered caretaker of the historical Golden Age, a '*Jack-of-all-Trades—wearing a perpetual smile*'.[6]

The abrupt shift from game-playing to the striking of a learned adult pose—Frank's parents are inveterate smokers and the cigarette was taken from his visiting mother's purse—captures Frank on the cusp of adolescence with a dual vision both child-like and something beginning to resemble adult sensibilities, an image of being that London was striving for in her early thoughts about the novel. In 2012, after some time away in Melbourne, London was back at her desk in Fremantle with a desire to write again, which she recorded in her notes for the novel:

> I am longing to write, to get on with it.
>
> Where to start?
>
> Frank arriving at the GA. What does he see? What happens? That above all. How does he make it interesting for us? What is interesting about this, for me?
>
> Being amongst children. Being able at once to be a child again, and yet see with growing comprehension. I have to re-enter the narrative again, connecting at once with the story.[7]

If the state London depicts in her first pages is Frank's childhood present and what he sees, then his past, which is narratively interwoven with the telling of his contemporary time, is also magically imagined with an ethical urgency and a profound sense of loss that Frank's parents carry heavily. As London's narrative relates, 'Sometimes he, Ida and Meyer said that they were a lucky family, because the three of them had survived and come to live in a free country' (51). The story of this survival is presented in a chapter of the novel, 'The Trains'—also the title of his Frank's 'most famous poem' (239), suggesting a later understanding of the shattering meaning trains carry for his parents—which is partly focalised through young Ferenc. It tells of him being sheltered as a very young child by Ida's infirmed piano teacher, Julia, and her resourceful partner, Hedwiga. Ferenc's understanding of why he is confined and quietened in an attic alcove when there is a visitor at the Buda apartment is represented as half-felt. His comfort in the sounds of the nearby train, juxtaposed with his observations of his mother's visceral reaction to the same sound—'Ida, he knew, shuddered at the sound of trains, which had carried off Meyer, and her father, and so many people she knew' (49)—brings London's readers to a devastating insight that Ferenc does not yet himself have.

However, this comprehension is carefully limited for the reader, too. The same chapter tells of Ida's determination for her son and husband to survive; with assistance, Ida obtains identification papers and goes to work as 'Terezia Bala ... a milliner from Szentendre, and, as from today, a house-keeper for an old couple. Suszi had given her a cross to wear around her neck and taught her the Hail Mary' (43) to earn money to buy food parcels for her husband that she hopes, somehow, to convey to him. Meyer's experience in the forced labour camps in German-occupied Ukraine are tellingly unrepresented in the novel; this absence is not an elision but rather a recognition that Meyer himself cannot narrativise neatly his suffering and loss. For Meyer, unbidden memories erupt and are displaced: 'He remembered his dream from last week. He was in the camp, in the Carpathian Mountains. Rain, rain he was saying, holding his tongue out. As if he was suffering from a terrible thirst' (166). If Meyer's memories surface through dream, then Ferenc's time of hiding is imagined, at least in part, in ways that are lifted from his storybook reading: 'He turned the pages of Julia's book from her childhood, dark paintings of goblins, forests, castles' (47). These are not stories that see maidens brought back to life with a princely kiss but rather are ones marked by horror and trauma. In the context of mass murder and disappearance which was the terror of Hungarian Jews, Ferenc's fate, and that of his family, would seem to realise the ostensible moral function of fairytales, namely that good triumphs over evil—not least aided by Hedwiga, a fairy godmother-like figure, who turns nettles into soup, finds milk in the face of privation, and 'always came back' unlike 'so many others' who did not return from their daily efforts to source sustenance (47). But the novel is disbelieving of such assured destinies and consolations, and gives to Meyer, in what might be read as the poetic free-verse form his son comes to privilege, the devastating lines:

> After he'd taken Ida home, he would go for a walk. Walk for miles and miles in the dark streets.
>
> He's lost belief that any one thing, person, country could be better than another.
>
> Szálasi had killed thousands of Jews, and all they did was hang him in their own terrible Hungarian way. (167)

Meyer's thoughts underscore that the moral surety fairytales promise has no secure place in London's novel.

If the moral certainties of fairytales are queried in *The Golden Age*, the novel nevertheless retains a sense of hopefulness. Meyer's wondering if a poet might be at work somewhere in the suburbs of Perth is a wish for the existence of beauty and understanding, and is also an expression of a quiet resolve to continue. This determination to endure is partly played out in the novel through Ida and Meyer's attitude towards Perth, the small capital city of Western Australia to which they take sponsored postwar passage and which is attributed a special charge in the novel.

The first sections of *The Golden Age* make it clear that Ida is physically and existentially displaced, and unimpressed by her new surrounds whose banal signs are taken as evidence of her resolute unhappiness: 'Every day, Ida found something that proved their voyage had been ill-fated. If she missed a bus, it was because they should never have come here' (14). Meyer, too, maps his exile and loss onto the streets and architecture of the city:

> If he didn't know better about human nature—his education has been swift and irrevocable—he would say there was an innocence about this city. Nobody there could imagine the waters of the Swan running red. The causeway bombed, tanks rolling up St Georges Terrace. Block after block of empty buildings, blackened and broken like ruined teeth. Shots ringing out. The hunted running through Kings Park. Bodies piled ten high on the steps of Parliament House … In an eye flash he saw his brother Janos pressed between other bodies, stacked up like firewood against the wall of a slaughterhouse. Janos no longer and yet, as Meyer stood there staring, for one moment, suddenly, vividly, Janos … (87)

That the city is not as innocent as Meyer believes is suggested by a passing reference earlier in the novel to the artwork adorning the office of the Golden Age. Determined by Ida, with her European tastes, to be 'kitsch', the pictures of 'Kookaburras and kangaroo paws and little naked black babies' (54) are less an aesthetic affront than testimony to the colonial practices and laws on which the city she now reluctantly lives was founded. Represented among the fauna and flora, the sovereignty and humanity of Indigenous people are unrecognised, as too is the colonial violence that displaced them from the land on which the city is built. For Meyer at this moment, however, the city is a site of psychic force and haunted remembering, and he spends much of the novel traversing its streets, first by foot and later as a driver for a local drinks company, as he also moves between his North Perth house and the Golden Age hospice to visit his recovering son.

It is in the streets of Perth that Meyer keenly feels his difference: 'It was a treeless road lined by offices, a government department, a warehouse. He would have liked to stop somewhere and have a drink … in a café with open windows: that didn't exist here. … he knew … that the bars in the pubs … were no place for a lone New Australian' (88). And his physical restlessness acts out his suspicion that 'never again would he feel at home as he once had. Never again on this earth. And another suspicion: that to love a place, to imagine yourself belonging to it, was a lie, a fiction. It was a vanity. Especially for a Jew' (87). London's giving to him the repetition of the phrase 'never again' underscores that Meyer's resolve is more than a private declaration. It also recalls most powerfully the shared injunction to remember, and not have repeated, the atrocities of the Holocaust, and subtly suggests that Meyer's individual experience, which the novel focuses on, is also nested in social remembrance and shared, catastrophic loss.

And while it would be a stretch to suggest that Meyer and Ida come to feel about Perth as they did pre-war Budapest—'the glamorous love of his [Meyer's] life' (86)—the novel does lead to a sense that 'What had seemed like the end of the world had become the centre' (152). These words, and the quiet realisation they herald, are Meyer's, and they are echoed some pages later by Ida at the end of a piano recital she gives at the Golden Age:

> Strange that this should be the moment that at last she fully understood. This was the land in which her life would take place. In which her music must grow. This was her audience. The émigrés, the petit bourgeois, the nouveau riche. Some country folk. She must do her very best. (168–9)

The concert is a fundraising event ostensibly held on the occasion of the Queen's visit, about which Ida makes her feelings clear: '"They've asked me to start with their awful anthem." Her hands began to block out the chords of "God Save the Queen"' (158). For Ida, her playing and commitment to European culture at first puts her proudly apart from all that Perth has negatively represented, and her agreement to perform after some years is a private note of thanks to whatever fortunes might still keep watch in her godless world: 'God did not exist. Tonight's performance was a thank-you note for Frank's recovery. To the Golden Age but also to Fate. They could not risk ingratitude ... Her art for Frank's survival' (156). Yet, the effect of Ida's performance is one of momentary connection that the music engenders, and which London's narrative represents formally, with the chapter that has her performance as its centre shifting and weaving between characters and their inner lives and their memories. One of the audience members is said to have 'felt a satisfaction, as if numbers were falling into place, something right clicking in his brain' (164) and this experience gives way multiply to compressed memories of one of the nurses; Frank's recollection, but not quite understanding, of his mother's heightened anxiety that he should learn to walk again—'You want to know why? They take the weak ones first' (165); regrets; and Ida's unexpected recall of 'Julia Marai, in the high attic room overlooking the Danube, shaking her head' (168). Each character is pictured as caught in their own thoughts; the music and the novel's structure, brings them into propinquity.

Even with this temporary closeness, it is not that Meyer's nightmares cease or the ghosts fade away, or that Ida can reconcile herself to 'Strange Australian rituals ... These thick floury breads that stick to the roof of your mouth. Breakfast food. And the peculiar custom of being invited into a bedroom to lay your hat and coat across the sagging marriage bed!' (227). Nor is it the case that the reach of antisemitism that shaped their lives so devastatingly in Hungary stops before Perth, so far away from Budapest. As one very minor character, Rodney Bennett, casually reflects when Ida rejects his suggestion that she play piano at his golf club: 'Weren't these New Australians always complaining about poverty? You'd think they'd leap at a chance to get ahead. Especially members of her race' (167). But Bennett's unthinking recourse to repugnant stereotypes and notions of entrepreneurial self-improvement is offered as the antithesis of the novel's contemplative and careful tenor as it attends to the specificities of Ida's, Frank's and Meyer's efforts to learn '[h]ow to live here' (211) in a future-looking present that is indivisible from the past.

The lessons the novel privileges to afford such querying are those that London gathers around another art form: poetry. *The Golden Age* is deliberate in setting out ideas about poetry it comes to value by staging a pedagogical scene that has Frank learning about verse in the hospice schoolroom. Mrs Simmons is the kindly teacher, 'clearly of strong character and intellect', who sets about instructing her pupil as a 'New Australian' on 'history and English literature' (74). In addition to memorising the dates of English monarchs, a timely exercise given the impending Royal visit but one Frank determines to be pointless and a sign of Australia's political immaturity, she hands out copies of Henry Kendall's 1867 lyric poem 'Bell-Birds' and tasks her charges with writing a short commentary on it.

With a colonial eye directed at Australian seasons, landscape and birdlife, Kendall's 'Bell-Birds' takes its cue from British Romanticism; the yoking of nature and childhood is caught by the first two rhyming lines of the poem's last stanza: 'Often I sit, looking back to a childhood, / Mixt with the sights and the sounds of the wildwood'.[8] 'Bell-Birds' became required reading for Australian students during the mid-twentieth century, and its canonical status is evidenced by the worn copies of the poem Mrs Simmons distributes and for which Frank feels some regret: 'It was cyclostyled in faint purple onto a yellowing sheet. Dozens of kids must have handled it. It was a shame to see a poem so stale and battered' (76). Even as the poem has been clearly overused in the schoolroom of the Golden Age, Frank takes seriously his teacher's commission; he tries to block out his noisy surrounds so that he might 'hear it' in his mind (76). He quickly determines that the words are 'lovely', but he soon has misgivings about their poetic presentation: 'he was caught up in the relentless rhythm, a galloping singsong. Those rhymes! That false arrangement of the words …' (77). In precocious protest, he tells his teacher that poems no longer need rhyme; in response, she defers to presumably unimpeachable tradition—'It's a famous Australian poem, Frank. Generations have loved it'—and issues the gentle instruction to identify its main themes in five sentences, with which he duly complies with a silent reservation: 'Mrs Simmons didn't understand poetry' (77). Frank's use of one word in an otherwise prosaic overview of Kendall's poem catches his teacher's notice, but she nevertheless confirms Frank's private assessment of her by failing to read the meaning of the look he gives in response to her question 'How do you know the word "nostalgia", Frank?' (78). Frank cannot, does not, answer. So, it is London's representation of Frank's internal response that gives shape and meaning to his glance, and which is itself a modest masterclass in the expansive possibilities of poetic cadence approaching the flow of thought that Kendall's poem cannot convey with its strict regularity of meter:

> He looked at her. How could he not? Nostalgia was everywhere. It had a special voice and special time—sunset, Sunday nights. It dimmed the light. Ida's *nostalgie. Nostalgie, nostalgie.* 'Gloomy Sundays', the Hungarian song that Ida played. (78)

Generations of musicians from Paul Robeson and Billie Holliday to Serge Gainsbourg, Marianne Faithful and Björk have heard in 'Gloomy Sundays' the melancholic note of love lost that Ida presumably perceived and obliquely communicated to her son with her playing. London's imagining of Frank's inner life in this way also, then, approaches in words the sound of an indeterminate, pervasive feeling that *The Golden Age* admits.

If Mrs Simmons' classroom instruction and syllabus are found wanting, it is not only because Frank has taken in his mother's longings and sadness. He has also been unexpectedly schooled in the potential of poetry by a fellow polio patient, although the reader's knowledge of this foundational experience is delayed by the novel's narrative structure. Before London's readers come to learn of Frank's time with Sullivan in 'the IDB (Infectious Diseases Branch of the Royal Perth Hospital' (5), an image of Frank, reposed, composing the first lines of poetry prompted by his feelings for Elsa, is given by London in the novel's titular, second vignette: 'A line ran through his head, which might be the start of a poem' (8). Frank's lines are ingenuous—'Your bed was empty today / when I looked for you. / Why?' (8)—although the concluding query might equally call to mind a wondering at Elsa's separate life; ruminations on his own actions; and metaphysical or existential deliberations. Moreover, this poetic effort sits tellingly at the end of the 'The Golden Age' section, which starts briskly in a manner akin to a medical report or welfare statement:

> Because he was so small and undeveloped for his age, Frank Gold, though nearly thirteen, had been admitted as a patient to the Golden Age. It was agreed, unanimously, … that it really wasn't suitable for him to stay amongst adult patients. Also, his parents were New Australians who both worked, and had no other family members to help with his care. He needed the nurturing atmosphere of the Golden Age, and supervision with schoolwork. Arrangements were made, almost immediately, and he was delivered there by ambulance that same afternoon. (5)

It is also in this chapter that the history of the Golden Age is offered, with its disembodied voice of bureaucratic efficiency standing in stark contrast to the fairytale register of the first chapter. The passive voice purports objectivity and benevolent authority, and there is certainly no room for understanding how Frank and his family find themselves in Perth. Nor is there the slightest hint that Frank is lately bereaved; that the passing of Sullivan, his poet-mentor, occurred before Frank's admittance to the Golden Age that near-begins the book. Instead, Frank's highly personal and poetical conclusion to 'The Golden Age' chapter is meaningful in that it gestures towards other forms of knowing that the novel esteems. Within this section's pages, London subtly stages the chapter's movement from objective to subjective knowledge by means of a doctor's prescription pad Frank finds in a carpark. This happened-upon stationery contains slips that would otherwise be 'waiting for its instruction' but Frank conceives of each instead as 'just the right size for a poem, or the first lines of a poem. For the words of your thoughts' (19). Direction gives way to the novel's preferred register of cogitation.

Yet, one of the lessons that Frank learns from his mentor Sullivan, and which London's novel takes seriously, is that for all its aesthetic and imaginative potential, poetry circulates in a world of material bodies. London makes this connection early in the novel in relation to Frank: 'Polio had taken his legs, but given him his vocation: poet' (8). Importantly, however, for a novel so involved with poetry, which by some measures turns on the connotative qualities of language in a way that dislodges from it the expressive responsibility language bears in prose form, London declines to turn the disease contracted by Frank and the other children at the Golden Age into an easy metaphor.

The novel is all too aware that the illness from which the children are recuperating will not only have long-lasting bodily effect; it also carries social judgement. When Elsa believes, for example, that 'She had brought shame on her family. People kept away from families of polio victims' (82), she is internalising an idea that echoes throughout the novel. By contrast, polio has brought Frank to poetry, and Frank himself, as an older man, somewhat sheepishly quotes from his own poetry to suggest that 'Polio is like love ... Years later, when you think you have recovered, it comes back' (240). Frank's simile carries with it a faint trace of the early-nineteenth-century Romantic poets, who associated heightened emotions and poetical creativity with their own historically specific affliction of pulmonary tuberculosis. And it also suggests that in Frank's mind, as well as his poetry, his early childhood experience of polio is entangled with his memory of Elsa, who (it must be said) does not provide Frank the regulation ending to the fairytale in which he first imagined her through the gap in the girls' dormitory door. Instead, as he tells Elsa's son, she 'met your father in Adelaide and got married. She wrote to tell me and soon after I left for New York' (237). So while London's narrative entertains these meanings that are attached to polio and the bodies it marks, *The Golden Age* meaningfully declines to treat the disease and experiences of it symbolically.

There is a realism accorded to polio, yoked with the historicity *The Golden Age* lays explicit claim to in its opening pages, and which finds expression in its unfailingly tender representations of bodies and their ministrations. The pains and significant discomfort the children suffer are recognised and respected—'The itchiness of sticky limbs inside the casts and splints could seem unbearable and the nurses took them in turn to cool down in the angel-bath' (126)—and the young patients' bodily capacities are celebrated, 'rumbling up and down the broad timber board on the verandah in the dusk' (126). In a very different but nevertheless related way, the highly likeable Sister Olive Penny, who oversees the Golden Age hospice and the children under her care, is presented as pursuing without hesitation the pleasures of her body: she is professionally benevolent and sexually assured.[9] And it is a commitment to sensuality that the other nurses of the Golden Age are implied to share but which Elsa and Frank are denied. The intellectual and physical intimacy that both child characters desire and understand as love—'he and she had received it very young' (187)—is abruptly ended by their expulsion from the Golden Age following the discovery of Frank in bed with Elsa and '[t]hey were sort of … undressed' (185). As a relatively enclosed world, the Golden Age has facilitated their attachment and hastened, or given expression to, their maturity. And while it might be that while in the hospice Frank's mind 'raced with the happy play of metaphors', as he casts himself as a romantic hero in a series of poems—'About the long journey he had made to find her. About the two devils, war and polio, that had brought it about, and the two angels, love and poetry, that had saved him. How Sullivan had showed him the way' (189)—these poetic ideals come up hard against the censure of the hospital's administrators.

If polio is not figuratively apprehended in *The Golden Age*, it is nevertheless tempting to read the exclusion of Frank and Elsa from the hospital with allegory in mind. After all, the Golden Age is a kind of paradise, separate and benign; Frank thinks back on the hospice and his three or so months there as 'an orchard of peace and light' (203). And while Frank certainly rejects any disgrace that might have been apportioned him because of his attempted intimate exchanges with Elsa, he is very much sent out into the world in the book's twenty-seventh chapter not as a romantic hero, as he might have once pictured himself, but rather as a mortal with self-knowledge of his human frailties: 'But he'd been away a year. He was taller, he had pubic hair. He'd outgrown his clothes, outgrown the need for his parents' attention. They hadn't yet learnt what he now knew, that he, and only he, could cope with his condition' (197). Insofar as the novel's readers are invited to note this allegory as well as others—London has Frank fleetingly identifying himself as the outcast Esau (203), referencing the representative struggle between the brothers Jacob and Esau in Judaic history and God's choosing of the former—in London's writerly hands Frank's expulsion is also a return. The chapter he is exiled to, as it were, is titled 'Poetry' and he finds in its world the abiding faith that poetry might 'save him' (197).

Before then, though, 'The Poet', the sixth section of *The Golden Age* whose title echoes that of the later chapter of exile, narrates Frank's unexpected apprenticeship to Sullivan; temporally, it predates the chapters that have preceded it. (Frank is transferred from the Infectious Diseases Branch of the Royal Perth Hospital to the Golden Age, but the latter institution is introduced in the narrative prior to the former scenes). This splicing of time is significant as 'The Poet' is one of the origin stories the novel affords Frank. The poet of the title ostensibly refers to Sullivan, who has just turned eighteen, but pertains equally, or at least anticipatorily, to Frank. Before encountering Sullivan in the iron lung ward, Frank has worn the mantle of 'The Kid' (22), the playful little brother figure who is living in suspended time: 'It was if he'd been given a reprieve from growing up' (22). But Frank's encounter with Sullivan is marked out as transformational; the experience is rendered in the fairytale terms that earlier chapters have established—'He'd entered another world with Sullivan, an enchantment' (27)—and which sets up the narrative as a part-*Künstlerroman*.

Before meeting Sullivan, if Frank had thought about poetry at all it was in terms that heightened his sense of difference. His parents' quoting of Hungarian poetry together 'set them apart from everyone else' (25). The element of magic Sullivan imparts to Frank is the revelation that poetry might be about the unremarkable, expressed in 'simple, everyday language' (25), contrary to both Ida's 'holy tone' (24) and the poems taught at school. Lord Byron's highly structured 1815 narrative poem, *The Destruction of Sennacherib* is singled out by Sullivan as exemplary of the kind of poetry that must be rejected (much like Kendall's 'Bell-Birds' at the Golden Age, which is noted later by Frank for its perceived shortcomings in the light of Sullivan's insights). With its Old Testament story of siege, war and murder, and God's almighty power, Sullivan holds up Byron's Romantic poem as demonstrating of all the qualities contemporary poets should shun, and is transformed by Sullivan into something juvenile: 'He chanted it fast, between breaths, like a nursery rhyme' (24). Sullivan plays to his agreeable audience of one, informing Frank of both 'new movements in the United States', among them, presumably, those that grappled with a determination that 'To write poetry after Auschwitz is barbaric',[10] and his own immersion in the First World War poets who, like him, wrote from their hospital beds.

For Sullivan, his illness marks a significant shift in his thinking about his chosen art, temporality and the (lyric) self. Polio has contracted and split time for Sullivan, with any fleeting relief from the disease 'just a reprieve' (31). He tells Frank that while he has always written poetry—'Friends. Sailing. The river in summer. Last day at school. That sort of thing. Nostalgia. Occasional poems' (25)—he now approaches it with an urgent immediacy: 'The poems are about the present. The past seems very far away' (25). This phrase drifts across the novel and finds itself with some variance in the mouth of Meyer: 'You know what, Feri? The past seems further away' (152). The shared refrain momentarily knits together two characters who never meet and who are referring to very different things. And this suggestion that poetical words might travel beyond the self, across time and distance, is repeated and caught in Frank's hope for his poems as an older man. They are 'in some way ... messages' to Elsa (234), he thinks, and they are answered in a way when Jack journeys to New York to meet his mother's childhood friend.

What provides the current for such hopeful connection is breath. Obliquely, London's novel is characterised by scattered but significant references to breath. As a child, Ferenc finds it difficult to breathe in the attic compartment of Julia's apartment (48) and he remembers how 'he, Meyer and Ida had been forced to live within breathing distance of strangers, like animals in a burrow' (56). In contrast, the children's breath at night at the Golden Age is imagined by London as 'light, cautious' (60); a revivifying breeze is said to have 'breathed cool life' back into Meyer after a day of factory work (85); and on the same walk Frank's father catches his breath in pride at the sight of the elite school to which his son has been accepted (89). Further, Elsa determines that that she 'only kept breathing because of her mother. So that her mother wouldn't die' (107); Ann Lee, a young patient at the Golden Age, remembers the 'hot breath' on her face of the horse to which she was unable to offer water due to her immobility (129); Ida readies herself for, and completes, her piano performance by an intake of breath; and on thinking of his 'wounded son', Meyer's 'breath hurt his chest' (205). When Frank and Elsa are momentarily reunited, it was '[a]s if the world was holding its breath' (230). London's novel seems to respire.

Most obviously and suggestively it is Sullivan, the poet enclosed in an iron lung, whose fragile breath is foregrounded in *The Golden Age* as both a physical action and a poetic possibility. In accordance with the novel's pressing concern not to render illness a trope, London draws Sullivan's circumstances realistically, as the recovering children at the Golden Age are also presented. Sullivan tells Frank, in good humour, for example: 'Can't pick my nose. Can't scratch my balls or wipe my arse. But apart from that, everything's pretty rosy, Gold' (29). Before this point, however, and by means of an introduction, Sullivan and Frank are pictured discussing poetry. In response to Frank's hesitant observation that Sullivan's own poetry, which he recites, does not rhyme as he expects, Sullivan's breath is emphasised graphically by London with ellipses.

Rather than marking out a pause or an omission, as ellipses are asked to do in the terms set out by punctuation convention, London has them signifying breathing: 'The poet smiled, breathed. "The Assyrian came down like … the wolf on the fold … And his cohorts were gleaming in … purple and gold"' (24). When he finishes reciting Byron's poetry to make a point about its accused traditionalism, Sullivan's breathing is again made apparent, the ellipses representing the labour of breathing with mechanical assistance. Sullivan tells Frank, somewhat imperiously, 'Look, Gold, Lord Byron wrote … that poem a hundred and … forty years ago. You don't have to … write poetry like that … any more. Good name by the way … Gold. Very … *apposite*' (24). What is most apposite, arguably, is that London, on Sullivan's behalf, tutors Frank (and therefore the reader) in a new way of conceiving of poetry, which is far less a theory than a way of living with poetry and polio, and of hopefulness. Rather than the regular stresses of poetical line that he views as conventional, Sullivan imagines a new structure and phrasing of poetry founded in breath. As London writes:

> If Frank sat there long enough, Sullivan would start to deliver a line on each out-going breath. Frank wrote them down in his prescription pad.

> It turns out that
> we are tough
> as cockroaches
>
> A shudder ran through Frank. He still felt too vulnerable. He heard the crunch of the carapace, the crack of fragile bones. Like all creatures, human bodies were easily wiped out.
>
> 'Don't worry, Gold,' Sullivan said. 'I'll work on it. The lung is a good editor.' (29)

Breath is central to this new poetry which has, as Frank part-understands, the potential, indeed the exigence, to be more than a matter of aesthetics. Frank's visceral reaction to Sullivan's poetic themes is an effect of his almost involuntary evocation of the Holocaust and, it is implied, the memory of being unable to breathe freely as a younger boy. But it is a response Sullivan misinterprets. He appears to read the younger boy's bodily quaking as a joinder to the new stylistic freedom he is advocating, unaware of the experience Frank brings to the poem-in-progress. Yet, it is a misunderstanding the novel's closing pages attempts to put right, or at least respond to, with Frank's visitor in New York, Jack, recalling a specific line from Frank's latest poetry volume—'All those I live with are unseen' (234)—that gestures towards the poet's influences and experiences. Frank, it would seem, has taken the lesson in poetry and breath Sullivan has offered him as a child and, as an adult, given it historical awareness and locatedness. Comprised of two elements, the line and the syllable, the living presence of absence is in the line's breath structure, which animates London's *The Golden Age*.

Conclusion

In the last pages of *The Golden Age*, Joan London has her poet-protagonist think, 'You never know who your readers are'.[1] The prompt for Frank Gold's reflection is the arrival at his New York loft of the son of the woman he knew, and loved, almost a half-century earlier when both spent months together at the Golden Age hospice during the Western Australian polio epidemic. Told in the present tense, Jack's presence collapses space and time, with Frank privately nominating the young man 'the Emissary' as '[h]e has come a long way, from a place Frank left nearly fifty years ago' (235). He is also Frank's ensuant reader; the poet had imagined Elsa, Jack's mother, as the intended recipient of his words but it is her son, an editor of a new literary magazine in Australia, who acknowledges the dispatch and travels to find out more about the poet who had been 'a presence in his mother's life' (233). The men share stories of Elsa and Jack asks Frank questions London might have fairly anticipated she would be subject to on the publication of that novel: 'Why is a book of poems about children in a hospital recovering from polio called *The Golden Age*? While acknowledging that this was in fact the hospital's name, was his use of it as a title ironic?' (237–8). It is implied that the poet eventually tells Jack what the readers of the novel already know about how Frank wrote his verse collection and Jack leaves with signed copies, a foretelling that he will not meet again with this frail man, and his curiosity met.

London's conclusion subtly unsettles the certainty Jack believes he has acquired. Frank, after all, admits happily that he is yet to complete the verse he inherited as a child from Sullivan, who died of polio in an iron lung, and which had evoked startling thoughts of the sublime:

> He felt dizzy; feverish. He was trying to finish a poem. Sullivan's poem, 'On My Last Day on Earth'. It was up to him. All around him he sensed the swirling rhythms of the hospital routine, the walkways like flowing arteries, the thick, breathing darkness of the rooms. And beyond that, the pulsing sun, the birds diving, the mysterious shadow life of the bush. He felt the living, throbbing world, and his own small beating heart no more than an atom within it. (34)

In the novel's present, Frank's repetition of these lines from the past in conversation with Jack—'"I'm still trying to finish the poem called: 'On My Last Day on Earth'." Frank smiles. "Still waiting on the final line"' (238)—calls forth the patterning that gives shape to London's narrative. The similar reiteration of the phrase also draws attention to its differences across time, with the introduction and repetition of the word 'still' signalling both continuation and a calm expectancy. As a child, Frank imagined poetry in terms of its necessary completion, and the thought was overwhelming. As an older man, he now sees Sullivan's guidance as having 'opened a door to a world where everything had meaning' (238) to which poetry is turned, but not definitively. It is perhaps no coincidence that on Jack's leaving, and to bring the novel to its end, Frank does indeed close his door once the younger man has descended the stairs, only to go 'straight to his window, just in time to see Jack's bright head enter the stream of the crowd and swiftly disappear' (240), with sibilance, and inconclusiveness, left ringing in the air.

Similarly, *The Good Parents* ends with an opening; Maya de Jong places a telephone call, '"Hello Andy," she said',[2] and the promise of a future response it carries closes the novel. *Gilgamesh*, too, concludes with what is imagined as Jim's beginning, 'The air shook and everything turned unreal. Passport, ticket, money, notebook: he stood on the verandah and checked his pockets, already in the traveller's world'.[3] And London's short stories are similarly wary of neat conclusions. In *Letter to Constantine*, Marc Chagall is pictured as staring uncertainly 'into the darkness of the skylight above him as if it is his frame';[4] following the 'first night' performance she gives with her friends in the story of that name, Jonelle Hughes in London's *Sister Ships* collection ends the narrative with an image of liminality: 'You had to cross the lawn with a steady forward tread, eyes straight ahead, just to get yourself inside'.[5] Jonelle's state of suspension is what London's writing in both short-story and novel form circle around, and a register on which they end.

This reflection extends to the two short stories that conclude *The New Dark Age*.[6] This compilation volume was released in the wake of *Gilgamesh*'s success and designed to introduce readers to London's earlier stories. It combines *Sister Ships* (minus 'First Night') and *Letter to Constantine* (without 'Pinch Me, Pinch Me') and includes 'The Photographer' and the titular story, which were published originally in 1996 and 2002 respectively. Both individually and together, this closing pair to the collection also resists any tying up of loose ends, the service to which conclusions are most often put. 'The Photographer', first published in the Fremantle Arts Centre Press collection *risks* (1996), edited by Brenda Walker, is bookended by two photographs that the text imagines into life as its female narrator, who travels in memory to her earlier life in Kalgoorlie, Western Australia, rides the Pittsburgh to Cleveland train, made restless by the Great Depression, and so continues the significance that journeying has for many of London's characters. And 'The New Dark Age', which appeared originally in Peter Craven's edited *Best Australian Short Stories* (2002), involves another of London's signature scenes: a group of characters, some at existential crossroads, who carry half-articulated regrets and deceptions; their futures, both shared and individual, are unclear.

Such characteristic open-endedness has particular significance for the narrative worlds of each of London's individual short and longer stories. But it is also a call to those unknown readers Frank Gold contemplates in the final pages of *The Golden Age* to return to what they have just read. London declines to summarise or tie up neatly her narratives, in part because these are stories of observation. These narratives do not exhort but rather register both the reality of the everyday and the complexities that comprise characters and their relationships. Further, this quiet refusal is also respectful of readers, who London invites to take part in the creation of her narratives' meanings.

This gesture is significant considering London's thinking about reading. London writes expressly of the pleasures of reading and re-reading in her introduction to the 2012 Text Publishing edition of Elizabeth Harrower's *The Watch Tower* (1966), which is now afforded the standing of a 'classic' (and serves as but one example of the shifting fortunes of Australian literature). London tells of how she came across the book randomly while seeking clues to her 'life and fate'.[7] With *The Watch Tower*, it is fair to say London got more than she bargained for. Not only was London introduced to an extraordinary novel and gifted an aesthetic legacy; she was also confronted with new ideas about Australian writing that welcomed, indeed demanded, other experiences of reading. As London tells of her first encounter with Harrower's novel:

> The novel gripped me like a nightmare. It had the strong, lively, unflinching writing of someone with a story to tell, who goes deeper and deeper into the characters, their feelings and motives, as the narrative races along … *I didn't know* … I remember thinking that. I meant: I didn't know there was writing like this, in Australia, now, by a woman. I read it as if it were a thriller, obsessively, though no one is murdered.
>
> …
>
> I never forgot *The Watch Tower*. The vision of the book, the sense of darkness in sunlight, stayed lodged somewhere at the back of my mind. I remembered the experience of reading it as intense, disturbing, though sometimes, in the sure hand of the creation of its villain, there was panache, even humour.[8]

Given this memorable impression, London presents her return years later to Harrower's narrative as edifying, with her re-reading carrying both 'the ghost of the first reading'[9] and the recognition that while words on the page do not change, a reader's receptivity to them does, freely admitting '[w]hat I had forgotten from my first reading, or perhaps was not ready to receive'.[10] London's readers might take their cue from London as both a reader and as an author, accepting her invitation to consider (for the first time, or again) what they too are ready to receive from her writing, on its own terms. Like Frank Gold, London cannot be sure who these readers are, and will be. But that unknown audience of London's work can be confident of meeting writing that is generous to the characters it represents and the curiosity and intelligence that is brought to the experience and pleasure of reading her narratives.

Joan London's Words

The last words of this volume are those of Joan London herself, an author with a sharp intellect who thinks carefully and seriously about her practice. From the archive, two pieces by London have been selected as representative of the preoccupations that thread through her long and successful writing career, which this book has sought to discuss. The first is a presentation given following the publication of her first volume of short stories; the second a talk on her first novel. Both pieces attend to London's influences, and what she presents as the responsibilities and pleasures of writing.

Why I write what I write[1]

This talk was given at the 1987 Warana Writers' Week, following the publication of Sister Ships. *London's ruminations on her coming to writing are illuminating, as are her thoughts on being a writer in Western Australia and the importance of writing to, and with, a vision sustained across her work.*

Writing, for me, didn't start to come together until about four years ago. Yet all my life, ever since I could read, I wanted to 'be a writer'. The ambition preceded the act by nearly thirty years.

Now I notice that this is quite a common phenomenon amongst women writers, that they don't get going until their thirties, or even older, and of course very often this late start has a lot to do with having children—what Cyril Connolly has called 'the pram in the hallway'.

But for many years, after childhood, not writing, not knowing what to write about, yet wanting to write, nagged at me in an underlying way. I felt its absence. I kept secret all my attempts. I was always looking at the biographical notes on the author at the front or the back of books, to see how old writers were before they published their first book.

For a long time when I was very young I thought that to write I would have to leave Western Australia. Books simply weren't written in WA I thought. They couldn't be. It was too flat and banal. There was no snow, or mountains, or villages or wars. Most of the books I read were English. I wished that I had been born somewhere else.

Also, as I grew older, I absorbed some of the puritanism of my upbringing. It wasn't a compliment to call someone 'arty'. It meant that they were pretentious, self-important, often silly. You were supposed to do something useful. I didn't doubt that books were useful, but I doubted that I could write anything useful. I didn't want to be pretentious. So that although I was 'good at' writing compositions at school—I saved up big words specially, I always put an adverb in after a verb, I got lots of ticks in the margins—I stopped saying so airily that I was going to be a writer.

Yet, in other ways my family life was a nurturing one for a writer. I was—am—the youngest of four daughters, the youngest by quite a few years so that my eldest sister was almost half a generation older than me. That four daughters are a literary hotbed was not lost on me—I was always trying to write imitations of *Little Women* and *Pride and Prejudice.*

By the time I came along, my parents were older and rather tired and left me alone a lot. I spent a lot of time *listening*, around corners, under tables or just keeping quiet in discussions, to stories and dreams of more grown-up worlds. Their lives seemed much more important and vivid than my own. Their worlds accompanied mine as a sort of precocious experience. I got used to the idea of myself as a spy, an eavesdropper. When my sisters were out, I tried on their clothes, put on their lipstick, clattered around in their high heels. I tried on their lives. My imagination was fired up by lives close to mine but not my own.

I also read their books. My sisters' books from their childhood had been printed during the war on special thin yellow paper with a special musty smell. These books had about them an atmosphere which I associated with Australia, like the dusty yellow light at the end of a hot day. It wasn't my Australia, it was the Australia of what I thought of as my sisters' more homely, more picturesque, post-Depression childhoods.

Our house was full of books. Orange and white Penguins, set school texts and school prizes, Reader's Digest condensed books. It was important that books were enjoyable or instructive. My mother advised me not to read *Wuthering Heights* because it was depressing. Art was meant to be cheerful, whether it was a print on the wall, or a film, or music. One of my sisters wanted to learn about classical music. She joined the World Record Club and played Beethoven and Rachmaninov on our radiogram. Someone always shouted 'Turn down that funeral dirge'. Yet the music affected me. It made me want to dance. I would shut the doors of the lounge-room and vaguely wave my arms around and thump about. For a while I thought I'd quite like to be a dancer.

I observed my sisters growing up in the fifties. I came of age in the sixties, with all that that means, in a much more dramatic, rebellious way. The particular path I took led me to living in a shack in the hills outside Perth for a year, and then in a farmhouse in a country town. This was regarded as a sort of apprenticeship to living on the land, communally, completely away from decadent society. The word was 'self-sufficient'. I remember heated debates as to whether this was 'opting out' or whether it was 'the only alternative'. The idea of it, if not the reality, captured my imagination for about four years.

Of course there are many reasons as to why part of a generation should start reading Krishnamurti, and a form a small movement 'back to the land'. I think of it as an offshoot of, and another form of, puritanism, searching for a new land, a new frontier. Although it was often germinated through reading, it was not conducive to writing, or reading, apart from the Vedantas or Herman Hesse. The main idea in those early flag-waving days was 'Be. Don't think'. I dismissed writing as a 'head trip', an irrelevancy, an 'ego trip'. All the same, I took notes.

Also the role of women in this movement, if properly carried through—I never got that far—seemed almost Biblical, toiling on the land, spinning wool, baking bread. There wouldn't be much time for writing. I took a note from a book that was being handed around at the time, called *Be Here Now* by Baba Ram Das, formerly Richard Alpers PhD. It was a sort of guidebook for mystic communes. He said:

> For the woman there will be the heavy pull of the earth element. The children will feel any psychic withdrawal on

> her part. When they wake up during meditation, explain clearly what you are doing. Do not sacrifice relationships with the children for what you may think is spiritual necessity. The whole thing is Sadhana. Sing together.

This was heavier moral instruction than I had ever had at home.

In the midst of all of this, I remember very clearly driving one night from our shack to visit some friends in their shack. We did not have electricity at our shack, but we did have a car radio. Suddenly, on the country road, I heard the beautiful measured tones of an American talking about why he wrote fiction. I found at the end of this talk that it was John Updike talking at the 1974 Adelaide Writers' Week. He said (I was later to find his talk in a book of essays): 'We must write where we stand: wherever we do stand there is life; and an imitation of the life we know, however narrow, is our only ground.'

We arrived at our friends' place, but I stayed in the car to hear the rest of what he had to say. His talk electrified me. A friend of mine, Witold Generowicz, who was later to make up and illustrate a children's book called *The Train*, once told me of a comparable experience. One day during his lunch hour from work, not really knowing what his next step in life was to be, he mooched off to a nearby railway siding and something about the empty lines and shunting carriages and signal boxes made him stand stock still with that same sensation, a sharp, prophetic stirring.

Eventually I came to write my first story. This was after my own true urban nature had reasserted itself and with great thankfulness I was back living in the city. I had also fairly recently had my second child. It was paradoxical that while

I was now very deprived of time by my children, they made everything more real. They made me accept where I was. It was a story ['Her Baby'] about a man with a baby. It was probably the easiest story I have ever written, one sentence following another, night after night when my children were asleep. I was surprised to find myself writing it, and completing it. I noticed that I felt very calm and peaceful as I did so. It was a great relief. Franz Kafka has called writing 'a leap from the murderer's row'.

I was very pleased with it at the time, but I didn't think of publishing it. I'm glad I didn't because now I can't bear to read it. I had to unlearn all of those ticks in the margin, all those big words and adverbs. After a while I wrote another one ['Old Friends'], and then another one ['Lilies'], which was published, in a Fremantle Press Anthology, and I knew that this was all I wanted to do.

All the same, when I did at last have the chance to write full-time—more or less full-time—I was very nervous. I had to give up my job and I didn't know if I could get it back in again. I felt I was putting myself on the line. Once again I found words of other writers very important. Elizabeth Jolley, in *Mr Scobie's Riddle* has a character, a Miss Hailey, a writer, of whom she says: 'Writing, she knew, even when it was what she most wanted to do, was an act of the will and as such required tremendous determination and discipline. She was afraid of failing to be determined and disciplined.'

About this time I had a dream. It was such a literary dream that it even had a title: Balmain Goes to the Haunted House. In this dream I found myself at a picnic with all the most contemporary Australian writers: those who figured in Frank Moorhouse's *Days of Wine and Rage*. The picnic was held in a beautiful old country house, said to be haunted. I found I was enjoying myself. I thought: this isn't too bad, everyone is very friendly, I am holding my own. But then night fell, and suddenly everyone had gone. I found myself alone in the Haunted House.

I think I have been very lucky, in that by the time I was writing seriously, and publishing, there were a lot of extremely strong Australian women writers, and this was inspiring and encouraging. I feel too that I have mopped up the benefits of feminist critics in my own acceptance of the essentially female content of my own work.

The act of writing, of making a start in writing, is often described by writers in terms of leaps. Eudora Welty has said that the writer 'took all that he knew with him and made that leap in the dark'. Virginia Woolf says: 'If you stop to curse you are lost … Equally if you stop to laugh. Hesitate and fumble and you are done for. Think only of the jump'.

It was only when I had finished writing the stories that make up my book [*Sister Ships*] that I noticed that the characters in many of them move in a physical way in the end, towards their destination. They scuttle, rush, climb, sometimes they even take off their clothes. They make a leap. I didn't intend this, I didn't know that the stories were going to be about acts of definition in a life. But I find it interesting that the book embodied the process of writing it. Stories show you where you are.

For of course, after all those years, I found that 'what one writes is based on what one is. One doesn't choose'. That's Philip Larkin.

To write one of my earliest stories, 'Lilies', I experienced what I suppose is called a 'flash of inspiration'. I was walking by a creek near a hotel that years ago had been famous as a honeymoon resort. Suddenly I saw a great sweep of arum lilies growing up from the creek banks. The combination of the lilies and the hotel came together in an instant in my mind for the germination of the story, which actually didn't turn out as I'd planned. Although ideas for my stories do not usually come as dramatically as that, I do need something to set me off, some people I see, something someone says, a memory. I have learnt to be alert to that prickling of interest, of possibility about something, something that I might not have expected to write about at all.

It reminds me of a game I used to play as a child. I used to take my blackboard off its easel and set it out on the ground and fill it with all sorts of objects, toys, ornaments, sticks and leaves for trees. I called it 'making a world'. I've seen a lot of children doing this, and then muttering to themselves, animating their world. What I remember is that sometimes these games got boring, they didn't hold my imagination, they petered out after ten minutes. Sometimes they took off, could take me in for hours. What was needed was something, something special that had caught my jackdaw eye, a little box, or a jewel, or maybe just a good idea from something I'd read. This is how I see the germination of a story, something that lights up for a little while the familiar, within the boundaries of its particular world.

What became important to me is to stay true to this vision, and to find the meaning in that particular situation. This satisfies in some way the puritan in me; it's a rather austere rational process of unravelling a puzzle, I find, of finding what is universal in human behaviour.

It no longer seems a disadvantage to still be living in Western Australia, where I was born. It is an advantage. It means that I am still surrounded by the sights and sounds of my earliest awareness. It means I have a chance to live amongst people I know well, and to see a pattern in their lives emerge.

I suppose it is not surprising that I wrote a book called *Sister Ships*, given my earliest environment. Again I didn't intend to call the book this: the story it is taken from is the last one I wrote for the book. For a while, I was going to call it 'Enough Rope', though I wasn't very happy with that, especially when I discovered that Dorothy Parker had written a volume of poetry called that in the thirties, and that a B-grade movie of the same name had recently been made. But then I came to that title finally, as I was writing the story, I knew that was what I wanted to call the book, that I had been writing about the lives of women, passing by one another, going their own way.

Writing has been a process of discovery for me: one of the things I have discovered was the importance of music to me. I have found it strongly connected to my work. When I hear some music, it reminds me of what I want to say. A story seems to me to have its own music, a refrain that is just out of sound. To get into the right rhythm of that story, to get its tone right, is to find its music. Sometimes such stories I write have an actual piece of music which I associate with it. Often that piece of music finds its way into the story. Yet I still know very little about music, I often can't remember the names of pieces of music, or identity the names of the composers. I am lucky to live with someone who loves music, and pursues it and plays it a lot. But in a way I can trace the thrill that some music gives me, and my response to it, wanting to move, wanting to dance, to the music one sister used to play, in the lounge-room, on the radiogram.

The Reusable Past[2]

Joan London gave this talk during the Adelaide Writers' Week in 2004. The piece focuses on London's first novel, Gilgamesh *and resonates with urgent concerns of the time, which continue today to demand recognition and restitution. It also thinks hard about the role of writing in the world. Here, London suggests that imaginative writing is a way of telling truths about the past and the present, and of giving pause to what cleaves us.*

As Samuel Beckett has written, in his characteristically pessimistic way, 'There is no escape from yesterday because yesterday has deformed us or been deformed by us'.

These are troubling times here, in which the old myths of the bush, the digger, the mate, the fair-go, however much they are touted in John Howard's Australia, are insufficient in the wake of the Stolen Generation Report, September 11, Tampa, Iraq, and the face of our compliance in a second colonisation, by America and American culture.

It's not surprising that Australian fiction writers have turned to the past to examine ourselves: that there has been a rush of historical fiction that some commentators have been worried about.

The first question I was asked two years ago by a radio journalist was if I thought my novel *Gilgamesh*, set roughly between 1918 and 1954, was relevant. My instant and instinctive answer was, 'Yes, or I wouldn't have written it.'

As Tolstoy declared of one of the great historical novels: 'What is *War and Peace*? … *War and Peace* is what the author wished and was able to express in the form in which it is expressed.' Because of course whatever writers wish to write is dictated by the present, by their current state of mind: consciously or unconsciously writers select settings the enable them to pursue themes and issues of relevance to their lives in the present.

What can be enigmatic is where the generating idea comes from to fix itself in the writer's mind: an image, a title, a dream, a memory, a historical event: a haunting that starts to take shape, becomes populated, a site in which many preoccupations being to be traced.

To me came first the intimation of a word, a faraway country among mountains during a time of war, and a myth, 'Gilgamesh', that took root in my imagination and which after many attempts began to find its form. I knew I wanted to join up Australia with that county and it takes the shape of a journey made by a young woman called Edith Clark, who grew up on a tiny impoverished farm in the South West of Western Australia during the Depression years, and who finds a way to cross the world in 1939 and reach Soviet Armenia, where she and her tiny son are trapped by war.

It wasn't as if I didn't ask myself, many times, what was the relevance of this tale, this journey, yet there was something compelling and entrancing for me about these images that I kept on pursuing, as if I were to discover its meaning through writing.

Much of the Australian part of the story was formulated in the area in which it actually takes place, the Margaret River area in the South West, now famous. There couldn't be a greater contrast between this playground of the rich as the South West has become, and what it was: an impoverished dairying area carved out of the tall timber in the 1920's by a government scheme called Group Settlement, in which a group of ten or twelve settlers, mainly ex-servicemen, English and Australian, were each given a parcel of land, twelve cows and a bank loan to pay it all off.

Edith comes from a Group Settlement farm: and I think this was a way to explore a fascination that I've always had with our pioneering past: what happened to those idealistic types who take up land and a way of life for which they are temperamentally unsuited, for those who are not practical, who live not through the work of their hands, but in their heads, and in books: the place of the, at least potential, intellectual in a rural-based society?

Edith's farm has been reduced to a home paddock, the rest sold off to a neighbouring hotel, the Sea House, which is based on a real hotel, still extant, in the area, Caves House where from the early 1900s, couples would spend their honeymoon, as my parents did, in the 1930s. And I think that in setting the book in its time-frame, I was exploring my parents' generation, a generation that lived through two world wars and the Depression, and the values of that time, of thrift, hard work, honesty, church and the lurking parental presence of the British, a presence that may have been resented or slavishly admired, but which was always there. These of course were all the values that had formed my generation and against which we rebelled.

I think there's always a certain edginess in writing of the past from the perspective of the present, that undercuts any nostalgia.

To write of the bush now, it's impossible to leave out the Aboriginal ownership of the land, their presence or the reason for their lack of presence, as was done in so many of the narratives written at the time. And impossible also not to mention and explore a little the unease in the relationship that white Australians have with the busy: a passionate love, but a sense of being an outsider: a distrust deep down of their right to belong there.

To have as a protagonist a young single mother is also a way to explore the narrowness, prejudice and puritan, often hypocritical values of the society of that time, the other side to that virtuous, hard-working generation. And Edith's lover is a dark stranger, viewed with suspicion in the little rural community. The xenophobia of that community is especially directed towards Edith's son, Jim, who has inherited his father's dark foreign features. He is bullied at school, as generations of migrant children have been bullied when they come to Australia. It's a xenophobia that's only been encouraged by the current policies of our current government.

Edith's dark lover is Armenian, a member of a race which suffered the first genocide of the twentieth century, when one and a half million Armenians were systematically murdered in Eastern Turkey in 1915 under the regime of Young Turks: a genocide for which many years went largely unacknowledged by the West and which the Turks deny to this day. Edith's trials as a penniless travelling single mother and her own experience of loss, are always implicitly contrasted with the vast, irrecoverable devastation of the Armenian survivors of that genocide. By the end of the twentieth century, we have become very aware of the trauma of the survivor and its reverberation down the generations.

And finally, in this bringing together of the past and the present is the exploitation of the myth of Gilgamesh, the oldest recorded poem in world literature: the very male myth of the arrogant young warrior king in ancient Mesopotamia, who sets out on a journey to find the secret of eternal life, and who returns home older and wiser and accepting of his kingly responsibilities. As Edith says when she's told this story: 'There's no place for a woman in this myth'.

Edith makes her journey with her young child, and she earns her way as a caregiver, a nurse. I wasn't interested in finding allegorical equivalents to the personae of the myth, or in a feminist retelling, but in testing how universal this myth was, why it has endured for three thousand years, and how it could be traced in all our lives: that is, the journey of a life from a youthful striking out, for fame or love or a place in the world, for some form of permanence, and then the hinge-point in this life, the return, the acceptance of death, of impermanence, the acceptance of who you are, and where you come from, and your own moment in myth and history.

Acknowledgements

This book was researched and written on Whadjuk Noongar boodja and the land of the Gadigal people of the Eora Nations. The Whadjuk Noongar people and the Gadigal people are the continuing custodians and storytellers of their unceded lands and waterways, and I respectfully acknowledge them and their elders, and their care of Country.

Melinda Harvey, the editor of the Contemporary Australian Writers series, astutely engaged with an earlier draft of this book; her feedback gave my ideas better shape. Catherine McInnis at Melbourne University Publishing provided practical assistance throughout and expertly copy-edited the manuscript.

I would also like to express my warm gratitude to Joan London and Geoffrey London. That Joan and Geoffrey affably welcomed into their home a (well-intended) stranger with a book to write is but one illustration of their generosity. Another is that Geoffrey beautifully curated Joan's literary archive, held in the Mitchell Library Special Collections, the State Library of New South Wales, which proved valuable for my thinking. Further still, kind permission has been given to reproduce Joan's published and unpublished words in this volume.

And Geoffrey read my manuscript with the greatest of care, for which I am deeply appreciative.

I am indebted, too, to my wonderful English and Literary Studies colleagues at The University of Western Australia for their camaraderie and intellectual generosity. Bob White's wise counsel and scholarly example are sustaining. My friendships with Paul Genoni, Victoria Burrows, Julieanne Lamond and Christine House are especially important to this book and to me. My parents, Margot and Kevin Dalziell, are unswervingly supportive. And to Jamie Hamilton and Eladia, Caleb and Jordi Hamilton-Dalziell: thank you.

Notes

Introduction

1 Julie Lewis, 'Interview: Joan London's *Sister Ships*,' *Fremantle Arts Review* 1.10 (October 1986): 11. A selection of short stories was reissued in Joan London, *The New Dark Age* (North Sydney, New South Wales: Random House, 2004).

2 Shirley Hazzard and Francis Steegmuller, *The Ancient Shore: Dispatches from Naples* (Chicago: University of Chicago Press, 2006), p. 13.

3 Alice Munro, front cover advanced praise, Joan London, *Sister Ships and Other Stories* (New York: King Penguin, 1988).

4 Charlotte Wood, 'Joan London,' *The Writer's Room: Conversations About Writing* (Crows Nest, NSW: Allen & Unwin, 2016), p. 224.

5 Charlotte Wood interviewed by Michael Williams 'Charlotte Wood Thinks Restraint is Overrated,' *Read This Podcast* 2 November 2023, transcript at https://www.thesaturdaypaper.com.au/podcast/charlotte-wood-thinks-restraint-underrated

6 Charlotte Wood, *Stone Yard Devotional* (Crows Nest, NSW: Allen & Unwin, 2023).

7 Elizabeth Webby, 'Literary Awards and Joan London's *The Golden Age*,' *The Conversation* 23 July 2015, https://theconversation.com/literary-awards-and-joan-londons-the-golden-age-44716

8 'Short Shrift: 2004 Adelaide Writers' Festival,' Joan London Literary Papers, Mitchell Library Special Collections, State Library of New South Wales, 9669448, MLMSS 11941, Box 19, Unnumbered file titled 'Authors' Talks, Eveline Kotai exhibition 1995 (incl. Kristeva and notes on exile), 'Writers Festivals 2003–2006,' p. 1.

9 'China and Australia: A View from the Bookshop [2005],' Joan London Literary Papers, Mitchell Library Special Collections, State Library of New South Wales, 9669448, MLMSS 11941, Box 19, File 5, p. 3.

10 Joan London, 'Introduction: The Only Russian in Sydney,' in Elizabeth Harrower, *The Watch Tower* (Melbourne: Text Publishing, 2012 [1966]), p. vii.

11 'Why I write what I write: 1987 Warana Writers' Week,' Joan London Literary Papers, Mitchell Library Special Collections, State Library of New South Wales, 9669448, MLMSS 11941, Box 19, Unnumbered file titled 'Author Talks 1, 1987–2013,' p. 5.

12 For an account of the early years of the press, see Per Henningsgaard, 'From Soundings to Yeera-muk-a-doo: The Early Years of Fremantle Arts Centre Press,' *Westerly* 54.1 (2009): 96–111.

13 'Somewhere Else: A Sense of Place: for *Theatre Arts* 14/9/1993,' Joan London Literary Papers, Mitchell Library Special Collections, State Library of New South Wales, 9669448, MLMSS 11941, Box 19, Unnumbered file titled 'Author Talks 1, 1987–2013,' p. 3.

14 Anon. 'Book of Dreams,' *The Age* 26 August 2002, https://www.theage.com.au/entertainment/books/book-of-dreams-20020826-gduj2x.html

15 'How Deep Does the Yellow Sand Go?' *Westerly* 29.4 (2002): 23. London writes of being a grandparent in the essay 'How Do His Clear Eyes See Me?' in Helen Elliott, ed. *Grandmothers: Essays by 21st-century Grandmothers* (Melbourne: Text Publishing, 2020), pp. 247–254.

16 'How Deep Does the Yellow Sand Go?', 23.

17 'Never Ending Story: Review of Alice Munro's *Open Secrets*,' Joan London Literary Papers, Mitchell Library Special Collections, State Library of New South Wales, 9669448, MLMSS 11941, Box 19, Unnumbered file titled 'Author's Talks, Eveline Kotai exhibition 1995 (incl. Kristeva and notes on exile), Writers Festivals 2003–2006,' p. 3.

18 'Alice Munro Tribute: October 2009 Vancouver Literary Festival,' Joan London Literary Papers, Mitchell Library Special Collections, State Library of New South Wales, 9669448, MLMSS 11941, Box 19, Unnumbered file titled 'Author's Talks, Eveline Kotai exhibition 1995 (incl. Kristeva and notes on exile), Writers Festivals 2003–2006,' p. 1, 2.

19 In her notebooks, London records Modjeska's assessment that the novel is 'wonderful' and notes how she herself is now 'excited/energised'. Untitled, Joan London Literary Papers, Mitchell Library Special Collections, State Library of New South Wales, 9669448, MLMSS 11941, Box 6, File Zl, unpaginated notebook 1995–1998. And in a letter sent to Modjeska, London made the impact and importance of her friend's intelligent involvement clear: 'I am very up and down about the ending. Too neat, too happy, too rounded off? … Any suggestions would be welcome, even a radical chop … Drusilla, your vision has been so important to this book. I hope it's not a disappointment. Yet again I send you my love and profound thanks'. As this note to Modjeska makes clear, it was the

last section of the novel, 'Return', that frustrated London the most, and which rippled out to the rest of the story. In earlier versions, and with the hindsight the published novel affords, this part is unconvincing. Untitled, Joan London Literary Papers, Mitchell Library Special Collections, State Library of New South Wales, 9669448, MLMSS 11941, Box 1, File Af, n.p.

20 William Maxwell, 'The French Scarecrow [1956],' in *All the Days and Nights: The Collected Stories of William Maxwell* (London: Vintage, 2012), p. 117.

21 Wood (2016), p. 248.

22 Charlotte Wood, *The Natural Way of Things* (Crows Nest, NSW: Allen & Unwin, 2015).

23 Nicholas Mansfield, '"The Only Russian in Sydney": Modernism and Realism in *The Watch Tower*,' *Australian Literary Studies* 15.3 (1992): 141.

24 Joan London, 'Introduction: The Only Russian in Sydney,' in Elizabeth Harrower, *The Watch Tower* (Melbourne: Text Publishing, 2012 [1966]), p. xiii.

25 Alongside these efforts to hold down thought are multiple drafts, both handwritten and typed, and plans for scenes; details for emergent characters, some of whom never find their place in final versions—Gina McCabe, a television presenter who escapes to Gilgamesh's Nunderup after a minor scandal in the city and who has a notebook filled with ideas dedicated to her, is one such character—and reflections on the pleasures and difficulties of writing. Additionally, London's notes are scattered with both reminders as to why writing matters and ways to keep going. Having commenced in February 1995 the novel that would become *Gilgamesh*, only then to change direction and start again the following year—'Beginning again. Armenia. Don't know what it is. A long story—maybe 40, 50 pages'—London writes for herself, as the novel moves into its third year and with no way of knowing that the first draft would be completed at the end of 1998,

> 1. Abandon the idea that you are ever going to finish. Lost track of the 400 pages and write just one page for one day: it helps. Then when it gets finished you are always surprised
> 2. Write freely and as rapidly as possible and throw the whole thing on paper. Never connect or rewrite until the whole thing is down.

'What can I see [?]' London asks herself throughout her notes, a querying that gives her pause and promises some future projection. It is hardly surprising, considering this archival trace of London's practice, that she should take a long time to write. Untitled (27/2/96), Joan London Literary

Papers, Mitchell Library Special Collections, State Library of New South Wales, 9669448, MLMSS 11941, Box 3, File Ao2, n.p.; Untitled, Joan London Literary Papers, Mitchell Library Special Collections, State Library of New South Wales, 9669448, MLMSS 11941, Box 3, File H, n.p; Untitled, Joan London Literary Papers, Mitchell Library Special Collections, State Library of New South Wales, 9669448, MLMSS 11941, Box 18, File 2, n.p.

26 Untitled, Joan London Literary Papers, Mitchell Library Special Collections, State Library of New South Wales, 9669448, MLMSS 11941, Box 18, folder 16, n.p.; folder 12, n.p.

27 Untitled (c. September 2000 – February 2001), Joan London Literary Papers, Mitchell Library Special Collections, State Library of New South Wales, 9669448, MLMSS 11941, Box 2, File Al, n.p.

28 'The Wrong End of the Telescope: Measuring Individual Histories Against Global Histories,' Joan London Literary Papers, Mitchell Library Special Collections, State Library of New South Wales, 9669448, MLMSS 11941, Box 19, Unnumbered file titled 'Author Talks 1, 1987–2013,' p. 2.

29 Wood, (2016), p. 236.

30 '4 women, 4 cultures, 4 Short Story Writers: 2004 Sydney Writers' Festival,' Joan London Literary Papers, Mitchell Library Special Collections, State Library of New South Wales, 9669448, MLMSS 11941, Box 19, Unnumbered file titled 'Authors' Talks, Eveline Kotai exhibition 1995 (incl. Kristeva and notes on exile), Writers Festivals 2003–2006,' p. 3.

31 Ibid.

The Short Stories: *Sister Ships* and *Letter to Constantine*

1 Joan London, *Sister Ships* (Fremantle: Fremantle Arts Centre Press, 1986). All references to this text will be cited by page number in the chapter.

2 Ray Coffey, 'Editor Notes,' Joan London Literary Papers, Mitchell Library Special Collections, State Library of New South Wales, 9669448, MLMSS 11941, Box 15, File 2, p. 3.

3 Joan London, *Letter to Constantine* (Fremantle: Fremantle Arts Centre Press, 1993). All references to this text will be cited by page number in the chapter.

4 'Short Shrift: 2004 Adelaide Writers' Festival,' Joan London Literary Papers, Mitchell Library Special Collections, State Library of New South Wales, 9669448, MLMSS 11941, Box 19, Unnumbered file titled 'Authors' Talks, Eveline Kotai exhibition 1995 (incl. Kristeva and notes on exile), Writers Festivals 2003–2006,' p. 1.

5 Ibid., p. 2.

6 'Never Ending Story: Review of Alice Munro's *Open Secrets*,' Joan London Literary Papers, Mitchell Library Special Collections, State Library of New South Wales, 9669448, MLMSS 11941, Box 19, Unnumbered file titled 'Author's Talks, Eveline Kotai exhibition 1995 (incl. Kristeva and notes on exile), Writers Festivals 2003–2006,' p. 8.

7 'Why I write what I write: 1987 Warana Writers' Week,' Joan London Literary Papers, Mitchell Library Special Collections, State Library of New South Wales, 9669448, MLMSS 11941, Box 19, Unnumbered file titled 'Author Talks 1, 1987–2013,' p. 7.

8 In 2002, Winton would reverse these fortunes, winning the Miles Franklin Literary Award for *Dirt Music* (2001) over London's *Gilgamesh*. Tim Winton, *That Eye The Sky* (Victoria: McPhee Gribble, 1986); Tim Winton, *Dirt Music* (Sydney: Pan Macmillan, 2001).

9 Quoted by Julie Lewis, 'Interview: Joan London's *Sister Ships*,' *Fremantle Arts Review* 1.10 (October 1986): 10.

10 'Somewhere Else: A Sense of Place: for *Theatre Arts* 14/9/1993,' Joan London Literary Papers, Mitchell Library Special Collections, State Library of New South Wales, 9669448, MLMSS 11941, Box 19, Unnumbered file titled 'Author Talks 1, 1987–2013,' p. 1.

11 Lewis, 'Interview,' p. 10.

12 Ibid., 10.

13 Kate Jennings, *Trouble: Evolution of a Radical / Selected Writings 1970–2010* (Melbourne: Black Inc., 2010), p. 13.

14 Lewis, 'Interview,' p. 10.

15 '4 women, 4 cultures, 4 Short Story Writers: 2004 Sydney Writers' Festival,' Joan London Literary Papers, Mitchell Library Special Collections, State Library of New South Wales, 9669448, MLMSS 11941, Box 19, Unnumbered file titled 'Authors' Talks, Eveline Kotai exhibition 1995 (incl. Kristeva and notes on exile), Writers Festivals 2003–2006,' p. 2.

16 Lewis, 'Interview,' p. 10.

17 'November 11th, 1975,' Joan London Literary Papers, Mitchell Library Special Collections, State Library of New South Wales, 9669448, MLMSS 11941, Box 16, Unnumbered file titled 'Burning Off Short Story Drafts, Notes,' n.p.

18 Lewis, 'Interview,' p. 11.

19 Gail Jones, *The House of Breathing* (Fremantle: Fremantle Arts Centre Press, 1992).

20 Gail Jones, 'Gestures Upwards: In Conversation with Joan London,' *Fremantle Arts Review* 8.7 (August/September 1993): 15.

21 'Keep it Short: 1992 Melbourne Writers' Festival,' Joan London Literary Papers, Mitchell Library Special Collections, State Library of New

South Wales, 9669448, MLMSS 11941, Box 19, Unnumbered file titled 'Author's Talks, Eveline Kotai exhibition 1995 (incl. Kristeva and notes on exile), Writers Festivals 2003–2006,' pp. 1–2.

22 Anton Chekhov, 'The Seagull,' in *The Cherry Orchard and Other Plays*, translated by Constance Garnett (London: Chatto & Windus, 1923), pp. 151–230.

23 Jones, 'Gestures Upwards,' p. 14.

24 'Keep It Short,' p. 3.

25 Perhaps this feature is why London wrote for her titular story a film treatment (which never made it to the screen), emphasising that 'These are essentially images from a mental landscape.' "Film Ideas", Joan London Literary Papers, Mitchell Library Special Collections, State Library of New South Wales, 9669448, MLMSS 11941, Box 17, Unnumbered file titled 'Letter to Constantine, drafts, film ideas paper', n.p.

26 Jones, 'Gestures Upwards,' p. 15.

27 Marc Chagall, *My Life*, translated by Dorothy Williams (London: Peter Owen, 1965).

28 This limit does not put an end to wondering, however. As she was thinking about the shape this story would take, London acknowledged in her notes: 'I can't get over, stop looking at, the portrait of my grandmother, Della Ward. Each time I see it I am more struck by her beauty. The string of Broome pearls, the puff of black hair as a pompadour, the faintly damp tendrils around her temples, her plump hands. The loneliness … about her face'. Untitled, Joan London Literary Papers, Mitchell Library Special Collections, State Library of New South Wales, 9669448, MLMSS 11941, Box 15, File 5, n.p.

Gilgamesh

1 Joan London, *Gilgamesh* (North Sydney, New South Wales: Vintage, 2001), p. 117. All further references to this text will be cited by page number in the chapter.

2 'Short Shrift: 2004 Adelaide Writers' Festival,' Joan London Literary Papers, Mitchell Library Special Collections, State Library of New South Wales, 9669448, MLMSS 11941, Box 19, Unnumbered file titled 'Authors' Talks, Eveline Kotai exhibition 1995 (incl. Kristeva and notes on exile), Writers Festivals 2003–2006,' p. 3.

3 'The Reusable Past: 2004 Adelaide Writers' Festival,' Joan London Literary Papers, Mitchell Library Special Collections, State Library of New South Wales, 9669448, MLMSS 11941, Box 19, Unnumbered file titled 'Authors' Talks, Eveline Kotai exhibition 1995 (incl. Kristeva and notes on exile), Writers Festivals 2003–2006,' p. 1.

4 Stephanie Trigg, 'Gilgamesh by Joan London,' *Australian Book Review* 232 (July 2001): 39.
5 'Tablet X: At the Edge of the World', *The Epic of Gilgamesh*, translated and edited by Andrew George (London: Penguin, 1999), lines 268, 256–7.
6 Charlotte Wood, 'Joan London,' *The Writer's Room: Conversations About Writing* (Crows Nest, NSW: Allen & Unwin, 2016), p. 243, 244.
7 Ibid., p. 244.
8 Ibid. pp. 244–5.
9 Ibid., p. 246.
10 The writing of *Gilgamesh* came out of not only dream but also a long writerly pause that followed the early successes of her short story volumes. As London's citation for the State Living Treasure award told of this period, 'the pressure of feeling obligated to create something new brought on a stagnant period for Joan. She grew fearful that she did not have any more stories to tell'. Department of Culture of Arts, Government of Western Australia 'Western Australian State Living Treasures 2015,' (Perth: Department of Culture and the Arts, 2015), p. 16.

On commencement in April 1995 of new writing, London recorded for herself on the first page of her fresh workbook her new determination: 'My new regime: to write a little every morning. Shower. Basic chores. Write for 3 hours, or until I can't go on any longer'. Yet three weeks later, London records her apprehension and the realities of being a writer with a family: 'Full of anxiety about everything and this is the killer of creativity for me … All I want is space to follow my vocation … I've 5 minutes or so—kids home, Jose [London's son, Joseph] to write his lit essay—needs my help. How to return to the deep dreams of Gilgamesh.' The next month she muses on an unattributed quote – 'The best thing you can do if you are the writer is to please yourself'—and wonders 'So what pleases me, how do I feel, see this novel. What is it I want to photograph? … If I were to write this as a film?' And three months later London is preparing herself for another attempt: 'Getting ready to return to this project. Must start all over again.' Untitled (14/4/95), Joan London Literary Papers, Mitchell Library Special Collections, State Library of New South Wales, 9669448, MLMSS 11941, Box 3, File An1, n.p.
11 'The Reusable Past,' p. 2.
12 'Telling Stories Over and Again: 2003 Perth Writers' Festival,' Joan London Literary Papers, Mitchell Library Special Collections, State Library of New South Wales, 9669448, MLMSS 11941, Box 19, Unnumbered file titled 'Authors' Talks, Eveline Kotai exhibition 1995 (incl. Kristeva and notes on exile), Writers Festivals 2003–2006,' p. 3.

13 '"Roam if you want to": 2003 Canada,' Joan London Literary Papers, Mitchell Library Special Collections, State Library of New South Wales, 9669448, MLMSS 11941, Box 19, Unnumbered file titled 'Authors' Talks, Eveline Kotai exhibition 1995 (incl. Kristeva and notes on exile), Writers Festivals 2003–2006,' p. 1.
14 'Tablet 1: The Coming of Enkidu', *The Epic of Gilgamesh*, lines 9–12.
15 'Roam if you want to,' pp. 3–4.
16 'The Reusable Past,' p. 1, 2.
17 *The Epic of Gilgamesh* itself shies well away from romance, with the arrogant (and possibly heroic, due to this fatal flaw) Gilgamesh rejecting Ishtar, the goddess of love, and her proposal of marriage. In the manner of great epics, the spurned Ishtar does nothing less than send a divine bull to destroy her would-be betrothed, albeit with no success.

The Good Parents

1 Untitled (12/11/01), Joan London Literary Papers, Mitchell Library Special Collections, State Library of New South Wales, 9669448, MLMSS 11941, Box 12, File 7, p. 1.
2 Untitled (7/8/98), Joan London Literary Papers, Mitchell Library Special Collections, State Library of New South Wales, 9669448, MLMSS 11941, Box 14, File 14, n.p.
3 Charlotte Wood, 'Joan London,' *The Writer's Room: Conversations About Writing* (Crows Nest, NSW: Allen & Unwin, 2016), p. 236.
4 'Why I write what I write: 1987 Warana Writers' Week,' Joan London Literary Papers, Mitchell Library Special Collections, State Library of New South Wales, 9669448, MLMSS 11941, Box 19, Unnumbered file titled 'Author Talks 1, 1987–2013,' p. 1, 3, 4.
5 Joan London, *The Good Parents* (North Sydney, New South Wales: Vintage, 2009 [2008]), p. 241. All further references to this text will be cited by page number in the chapter.
6 Writing of those phenomena as markers of 'now' anticipates future comment on their obsolescence and their roles as markers of a particular time.
7 Wood (2016), p. 234–5.

The Golden Age

1 Joan London, *The Golden Age* (North Sydney, New South Wales: Vintage, 2014), p. 153. All further references to this text will be cited by page number in the chapter.
2 John H. Smith, 'Fear, frustration and the will to overcome: A social history of poliomyelitis in Western Australia,' PhD thesis (History), Edith Cowan University, 1997, p. 27.

3 Joan London, 'Interview: 2015 Adelaide Writers' Week,' https://youtu.be/9S2p8EkSxJ8 (accessed July 2023).
4 Neither was the writing of the novel as easy as London makes it sound. In her notebooks focused on the novel, she reminds herself of 'The Right to Write', and records moments of distress and hesitation; the writing down of which seems a way to recognise and think through the anxiety: 'What is it I have to say? What is it I must write? Only this. Frank's Folly. Over and over. Where to start? With light again. Over and over I must keep in touch with what is important. CALM DOWN'. Untitled (c. February 2012), Joan London Literary Papers, Mitchell Library Special Collections, State Library of New South Wales, 9669448, MLMSS 11941, Box 9, File 30, n.p.
5 Helen Garner, 'Launch of *The Good Parents*' (8 August 2014), Joan London Literary Papers, Mitchell Library Special Collections, State Library of New South Wales, 9669448, MLMSS 11941, Box 10, File 35, p. 1.
6 Joy Hornidge, *Looking Back on the 'Golden Age* (Subiaco: Post Polio Network of Western Australia, 2005), p. 6.
7 'Home' (5 March 2012), Joan London Literary Papers, Mitchell Library Special Collections, State Library of New South Wales, 9669448, MLMSS 11941, Box 9, Item 28, n.p.
8 Henry Kendall, 'Bell-Birds' in *Leaves from Australian Forests* (Melbourne: George Roberstson, 1869), p. 47.
9 Sister Penny is one of London's most joyous creations. As Helen Garner noted in her launch speech: 'The matron of the convalescent hospital is a splendid piece of work. The way Joan London creates Sister Penny's efficiently and discreetly ordered sex life is a miracle of subtlety'. Garner, 'Launch of *The Good Parents*,' p. 3.
10 Theodor W Adorno, 'Culture, Criticism and Society,' in *Prisms*, translated by Samuel and Shierry Weber (Cambridge, Massachusetts: MIT Press, 1983 [1967]), p. 34.

Conclusion

1 Joan London, *The Golden Age* (North Sydney, New South Wales: Vintage, 2014), p. 236. All further references to this text will be cited by page number in the chapter.
2 Joan London, *The Good Parents* (North Sydney, New South Wales: Vintage, 2009 [2008]), p. 349.
3 Joan London, *Gilgamesh* (North Sydney, New South Wales: Vintage, 2001), p. 256.
4 Joan London, *Letter to Constantine* (Fremantle: Fremantle Arts Centre Press, 1993), p. 102.

5 Joan London, *Sister Ships* (Fremantle: Fremantle Arts Centre Press, 1986), p. 42.
6 Joan London, *The New Dark Age* (North Sydney, New South Wales: Random House, 2004).
7 Joan London, 'Introduction: The Only Russian in Sydney,' in Elizabeth Harrower, *The Watch Tower* (Melbourne: Text Publishing, 2012 [1966]), p. vii.
8 Ibid., p. viii, xi.
9 Ibid., p. xi.
10 Ibid., p. xii.

Joan London's Words

1 'Why I write what I write: 1987 Warana Writers' Week,' Joan London Literary Papers, Mitchell Library Special Collections, State Library of New South Wales, 9669448, MLMSS 11941, Box 19, Unnumbered file titled 'Author Talks 1, 1987–2013, pp. 1–8.
2 'The Reusable Past: 2004 Adelaide Writers' Festival,' Joan London Literary Papers, Mitchell Library Special Collections, State Library of New South Wales, 9669448, MLMSS 11941, Box 19, Unnumbered file titled 'Authors' Talks, Eveline Kotai exhibition 1995 (incl. Kristeva and notes on exile), Writers Festivals 2003–2006,' pp. 1–3.

THE MIEGUNYAH PRESS

This book was designed and typeset
by Cannon Typesetting
The text was set in 11¼ point Adobe Caslon Pro
with 15 points of leading
The text is printed on 70gsm book white
This book was edited by Catherine McInnis